Web Design Blueprint

A Practical Guide to Modern Web Creation

By Miles B. Wilson

Table of contents

Introduction

Chapter 1: Web Design Fundamentals

Chapter 2: Core Web Technologies: HTML

Chapter 3: Styling with CSS

Chapter 4: Responsive Design and Layouts

- 4.1: Responsive Design Principles and Techniques

- 4.2: Media Queries and Breakpoint Implementation

- 4.3: Flexible Layouts: Flexbox and Grid

Chapter 5: Enhancing Interactivity with JavaScript

- 5.1: JavaScript Basics: Variables, Functions, DOM

- 5.2: Event Handling and Dynamic Content

- 5.3: Interactive UI Elements: Modals, Sliders, etc.

Chapter 6: The Modern Web Design Workflow

- 6.1: User-Centered Design: Research and Planning

- 6.2: Wireframing, Prototyping, and Iteration

- 6.3: Accessibility and Performance Optimization

Chapter 7: Advanced CSS and JavaScript Techniques

- 7.1: CSS Preprocessors and Animations

- 7.2: Advanced JavaScript: Asynchronous Operations

- 7.3: Introduction to Frameworks (Optional Overview)

Chapter 8: Practical Application: Building a Website

Chapter 9: Emerging Trends and Best Practices

Conclusion

Introduction: Your Journey into Web Design

Welcome to "Web Design Blueprint." I'm thrilled to have you join me on this journey into the exciting and ever-evolving world of creating websites. Whether you've always dreamed of building your own online portfolio, launching an e-commerce store, or simply understanding the magic behind the websites you visit every day, you're in the right place.

Why Web Design Matters

In today's digital age, the web is where we connect, learn, and do business. A well-designed website isn't just a pretty face; it's a powerful tool that can communicate your message, build your brand, and achieve your goals. Think of it as your digital storefront, your online resume, or your personal creative outlet.

My Own Web Design Story

I remember when I first started exploring web design. It felt like diving into a vast ocean of code and design principles. Honestly, it was a bit overwhelming! I spent countless hours experimenting, making mistakes, and learning from those mistakes. There were moments of frustration, but also moments of pure excitement when I saw my creations come to life.

One of the biggest lessons I learned was that web design is a blend of technical skills and creative thinking. It's about understanding the logic of code, but also about having an eye for aesthetics and a passion for creating engaging user experiences.

What This Book Offers

This book is designed to be your friendly guide, breaking down complex concepts into easy-to-understand steps. We'll start with the fundamentals of HTML, CSS, and JavaScript, and gradually move on to more advanced techniques like responsive design, interactivity, and design workflows.

Here's what you can expect:

- **Practical, Hands-On Approach:** We'll focus on building real-world projects, so you can apply what you learn.
- **Clear and Concise Explanations:** I'll explain technical concepts in plain language, avoiding jargon whenever possible.
- **Visual Examples and Code Snippets:** You'll see plenty of examples to illustrate the concepts we cover.
- **Personal Insights and Tips:** I'll share my own experiences and lessons learned along the way.
- **A Focus on Modern Web Design:** We'll cover the latest trends and best practices in the industry.

Who This Book Is For

This book is for anyone who wants to learn web design, regardless of their prior experience. Whether you're a complete beginner, a student, or a professional looking to expand your skills, you'll find valuable information and practical guidance here.

What You'll Learn

By the end of this book, you'll be able to:

- Understand the core principles of web design.
- Build websites using HTML, CSS, and JavaScript.
- Create responsive layouts that adapt to different devices.
- Design interactive user interfaces.
- Apply modern design workflows and best practices.

- Understand the importance of accessibility and performance.

Let's Get Started!

Web design is a journey of continuous learning and exploration. There's always something new to discover and something to improve. So, grab your favorite text editor, fire up your browser, and let's dive in.

Chapter 1: Web Design Fundamentals

Whether you're a complete beginner or looking to refresh your knowledge, this chapter lays the groundwork for creating stunning and effective websites. We'll explore the core principles, essential design elements, and the tools you'll need to get started.

1.1: Defining Web Design: UX/UI Principles

So, we're talking about web design. But what does that *really* mean? It's not just slapping some colors and pictures onto a screen. It's about creating a digital experience that's both functional and delightful. At the heart of this lie UX and UI.

Understanding the Core: UX and UI

Think of web design as building a house. You need a solid foundation, a functional layout, and a pleasing aesthetic. That's where UX and UI come in.

- **User Experience (UX): The Feeling of Interaction**
  - UX focuses on the user's *overall experience* when interacting with a website.It's about how they feel, how easily they can navigate, and whether they can achieve their goals.
  - Key aspects include usability, accessibility, and overall satisfaction.
  - Essentially, UX designers ask: "Is this website easy and enjoyable to use?"

Personal Insight: Early on, I'd get caught up in the visuals, forgetting about the user's journey. I'd built sites that looked great, but were a pain to navigate. That's when I grasped the importance of UX. A site with a poor UX will drive users away, regardless of how good it looks.

- **User Interface (UI): The Visual Gateway**
  - UI deals with the *visual elements* of a website – buttons, menus, icons, and layout. It's about how the user interacts with the interface.
  - Key aspects include visual design, interaction design, and information architecture.
  - UI designers ask: "Is this website visually appealing and intuitive?"
  - Think of UI as the bridge between the user and the website's functionality. It must be clear, consistent, and visually engaging.

The Symbiotic Relationship

UX and UI are not separate entities; they're two sides of the same coin. A great UI without good UX is like a beautiful house with a terrible floor plan. Similarly, excellent UX with a poor UI is like a well-designed house that's falling apart visually.

- **How They Intertwine:**
  - A well-designed UI enhances the UX by making the website easy to navigate and visually appealing.
  - A strong UX informs the UI by ensuring that the design elements are functional and user-friendly.

Key Principles to Consider

- **User-Centered Design:** Always put the user first.Understand their needs, goals, and behaviors.
- **Simplicity and Clarity:** Avoid clutter and use clear, concise language.
- **Consistency:** Maintain a consistent design language throughout the website.
- **Accessibility:** Design for users with disabilities.
- **Feedback and Iteration:** Gather user feedback and continuously improve the design.

The Impact of Good UX/UI

- **Increased User Engagement:** Users are more likely to stay on a website that's easy and enjoyable to use.
- **Improved Conversion Rates:** A well-designed website can increase the likelihood of users taking desired actions.
- **Enhanced Brand Reputation:** A positive user experience can strengthen your brand's reputation.
- **Reduced Support Costs:** A user-friendly website can reduce the need for customer support.

In essence, web design is about creating a seamless and enjoyable experience for the user. By understanding and applying UX/UI principles, you can build websites that are not only visually appealing but also highly effective.

1.2: Design Essentials: Color, Typography, Layout

These three elements are the visual backbone of any website. They dictate how users perceive and interact with your content.Let's explore each in detail.

Color: Setting the Mood and Guiding the Eye

Color is more than just decoration; it's a powerful tool for communication and emotional connection.

- **Psychology of Color:**
  - Different colors evoke different emotions. For example, blue often conveys trust and stability, while red can signify excitement or urgency.
  - Consider your target audience and the message you want to convey when choosing a color palette.
- **Color Harmony:**

- Use color palettes that are visually pleasing and harmonious. Tools like Adobe Color or Coolors can help you generate effective palettes.
- Remember the 60-30-10 rule: 60% primary color, 30% secondary color, 10% accent color.
- **Accessibility:**
  - Ensure sufficient color contrast between text and background for readability, especially for users with visual impairments.

Personal Insight: I've learned the hard way about contrast. I once designed a site with light gray text on a slightly darker gray background. It looked "subtle" to me, but was unreadable for many. Always check your contrast ratios!

Typography: Communicating Clearly and Effectively

Typography is about choosing and arranging typefaces to make written content legible and visually appealing.

- **Readability and Legibility:**
  - Choose typefaces that are easy to read on screens. Sans-serif fonts are often preferred for body text, while serif fonts can be used for headings.
  - Pay attention to font size, line height, and letter spacing.
- **Hierarchy:**
  - Use different font sizes and weights to create a visual hierarchy and guide the reader's eye.
  - Headings should be larger and bolder than body text.
- **Consistency:**
  - Maintain consistency in font choices and styles throughout the website.

Personal Insight: I used to think more fonts meant more creativity. Now I know sticking to a maximum of 2-3 font families creates better visual harmony and a more professional look.

Layout: Structuring Content for Clarity and Navigation

Layout is about arranging content elements on the page to create a clear and organized structure.

- **Grid Systems:**
    - Use grid systems to create a consistent and balanced layout.
    - Grid systems help align elements and create visual rhythm.
- **White Space:**
    - Use white space (negative space) to create visual breathing room and improve readability.
    - White space helps separate content elements and reduce clutter.
- **Visual Hierarchy:**
    - Arrange elements in a way that guides the user's eye to the most important content.
    - Use size, color, and placement to create a visual hierarchy.
    - **Personal Insight:** I used to cram as much information onto the page as possible. Now, I understand the value of white space. It not only makes the page look cleaner, but also helps users focus on the key information.

The Interplay of Elements

These three elements work together to create a cohesive and effective design.

- **Color and Typography:** Color can be used to highlight important text elements and create visual interest.
- **Typography and Layout:** Typography choices can influence the layout and vice versa.

- **Color and Layout:** Color can be used to create visual separation and guide the user's eye through the layout.

1.3: Development Environment: Tools and Setup

Building websites requires the right tools. Think of it like a carpenter needing a hammer and saw. We need our digital equivalents.

The Essential Toolkit

- **Text Editor: Your Code's Canvas**
    - This is where you'll write your HTML, CSS, and JavaScript.
    - **Popular Choices:**
        - **Visual Studio Code (VS Code):** My top recommendation. It's free, powerful, and has a vast library of extensions. Extensions can supercharge your coding.
        - **Sublime Text:** Fast and lightweight, known for its speed.
        - **Atom:** Highly customizable, but now archived.
    - **Expert Commentary:** Choosing a text editor is a personal preference. Try a few and see what feels right.
    - **Personal Insight:** I used to bounce between editors, but VS Code's extensions and integrated terminal have made it my go-to. The ability to debug directly in the editor is a huge time-saver.
- **Web Browser: Your Live Preview**
    - You'll need a modern browser to view and test your websites.
    - **Recommended Browsers:**
        - **Chrome:** Excellent developer tools.
        - **Firefox:** Strong on privacy and developer features.
        - **Edge:** Constantly improving, also has strong developer tools.
    - **Developer Tools:** These are built-in tools that allow you to inspect and debug your code. You'll be using these *constantly*.

Personal Insight: Learning to use the browser's developer tools is like getting X-ray vision for your website. You can see exactly what's going on under the hood.

- **Design Software (Optional): Visualizing Your Ideas**
    - If you're working with visual designs, these tools are helpful for creating mockups and prototypes.
    - **Popular Options:**
        - **Figma:** Cloud-based, great for collaboration, and has a very useful free tier.
        - **Adobe XD:** Part of the Adobe Creative Cloud, good for prototyping.
        - **Sketch (macOS only):** Popular among UI/UX designers.
    - **Expert Commentary:** If you're focusing on code, you might not need these tools. But if you're involved in the design process, they're essential.
- **Local Server (Optional): Simulating a Real Environment**
    - For dynamic websites or projects with server-side code, a local server is essential.
    - **Popular Options:**
        - **XAMPP/MAMP:** Bundles of Apache, MySQL, and PHP.
        - **Node.js with** http-server **or** live-server: Lightweight options for static sites.
    - **Expert Commentary:** For beginners, a local server might be overkill. But as you progress, you'll find it invaluable.

Setting Up Your Environment: A Step-by-Step Guide

1. **Install a Text Editor:** Download and install your preferred text editor.
2. **Install a Web Browser:** Ensure you have a modern web browser installed.
3. **Explore Developer Tools:** Familiarize yourself with your browser's developer tools. Right click on any webpage and select "inspect" or "inspect element".

4. **Create a Project Folder:** Create a dedicated folder for your web design projects. This keeps your files organized.

5. **Optional: Install Design Software:** If you'll be working with visual designs, install the necessary software.

6. **Optional: Set Up a Local Server:** If you'll be working with dynamic websites, set up a local server.

Key Considerations

- **Operating System:** Choose tools that are compatible with your operating system.
- **Workflow:** Consider your workflow and choose tools that enhance your productivity.
- **Community Support:** Choose tools with a strong community for support and resources.

Chapter 2: Core Web Technologies: HTML

We're going to dive into the bedrock of web development: HTML. Think of HTML as the skeleton of your website – it provides the structure and content that everything else builds upon.

2.1: HTML Structure and Semantics

HTML is the backbone of every webpage. It provides the structure and meaning to your content.But it's not just about throwing tags together; it's about creating a well-organized and meaningful document.

The Basic HTML Structure: The Skeleton

Every HTML document follows a specific structure, like the frame of a house.

1. <!DOCTYPE html>:
   - This declaration tells the browser which version of HTML you're using.For HTML5, it's simply <!DOCTYPE html>.
   - It should be the very first line of your HTML document.
2. <html>:
   - The root element of the HTML page. Everything else goes inside this tag.
   - It defines the beginning and end of the HTML document.
3. <head>:
   - Contains metadata about the HTML document. This includes things like the title, character set, and links to stylesheets.
   - Content in the <head> is not displayed on the page itself.
4. <body>:
   - Contains the visible content of the HTML page. This is what users see in their browsers.

Example: A Basic HTML Document

HTML

- `<!DOCTYPE html>`
- `<html>`
- `<head>`
- `<title>My First Semantic Page</title>`
- `<meta charset="UTF-8">`
- `</head>`
- `<body>`
- `<header>`
- `<h1>Welcome to My Website</h1>`
- `<nav>`
- `<ul>`
- `<li><a href="#">Home</a></li>`
- `<li><a href="#">About</a></li>`
- `<li><a href="#">Contact</a></li>`
- `</ul>`
- `</nav>`
- `</header>`
- `<main>`
- `<article>`
- `<h2>My Latest Article</h2>`
- `<p>This is the content of my article.</p>`
- `</article>`
- `</main>`
- `<footer>`
- `<p>&copy; 2024 My Website</p>`
- `</footer>`
- `</body>`

o   </html>

Semantic HTML: Giving Meaning to Structure

Semantic HTML is about using HTML tags that accurately describe the meaning of the content. This makes your code more readable, accessible, and SEO-friendly.

- **Why Semantics Matter:**
    - **Accessibility:** Screen readers and assistive technologies rely on semantic HTML to understand the structure and content of a webpage.
    - **SEO:** Search engines use semantic HTML to understand the context of your content, which can improve your search rankings.
    - **Maintainability:** Semantic HTML makes your code easier to read and maintain.
- **Key Semantic Elements:**
    - <header>: Represents the header of a section or page.
    - <nav>: Represents a section of navigation links.
    - <main>: Represents the main content of the document.
    - <article>: Represents a self-contained composition (e.g., a blog post).
    - <section>: Represents a thematic grouping of content.
    - <aside>: Represents content that is tangentially related to the main content.
    - <footer>: Represents the footer of a section or page.

Practical Implementation: Step-by-Step

1. **Start with the Basic Structure:** Create a new HTML file and add the <!DOCTYPE html>, <html>, <head>, and <body> tags.
2. **Add Metadata:** In the <head> section, add a <title> tag and a <meta charset="UTF-8"> tag. The meta tag ensures your site can display many different characters.

3. **Structure the Content:** Use semantic HTML tags to structure your content. For example, use <header>, <nav>, <main>, <article>, and <footer>.

4. **Add Content:** Add your content inside the appropriate semantic tags.

5. **Test Your Code:** Open your HTML file in a web browser to see the results.

Expert Commentary and Personal Insights:

- **Avoid <div> Soup:** While <div> tags are useful, overuse can lead to "div soup," making your code difficult to read and maintain. Use semantic tags whenever possible.

- **Accessibility First:** Always consider accessibility when writing HTML. Semantic HTML is a crucial part of creating accessible websites.

- **Personal Insight:** I remember when I first started, I used <div> tags for everything. It worked, but my code was a mess. Learning semantic HTML made my code cleaner, more organized, and more accessible.Now, I always try to use the most appropriate semantic tag for each piece of content.

2.2: Essential HTML Elements and Attributes

HTML elements are the building blocks of web pages. Attributes provide additional information about those elements. Let's explore the most crucial ones.

Essential HTML Elements: The Bricks and Mortar

1. **Headings (<h1> to <h6>):**
   - Used to define headings of different levels. <h1> is the most important heading, and <h6> is the least.
   - **Example:**

HTML

- <h1>Main Heading</h1>
- <h2>Subheading</h2>
- <h3>Section Heading</h3>
- **Expert Commentary:** Use headings to create a clear hierarchy of information. Don't skip heading levels (e.g., go from <h1> to <h3>).

2. **Paragraphs (<p>):**
    - Used to define paragraphs of text.
    - **Example:**

HTML

- <p>This is a paragraph of text. It contains information that is displayed to the user.</p>
    - **Personal Insight:** I used to put all my text in one giant paragraph. Breaking it into smaller paragraphs makes it much easier to read.

3. **Links (<a>):**
    - Used to create hyperlinks to other web pages or resources.
    - The href attribute specifies the URL.
    - **Example:**

HTML

- <a href="https://www.example.com">Visit Example Website</a>

- **Expert Commentary:** Use descriptive link text to improve accessibility and SEO.

4. **Images (<img>):**
   - Used to embed images in a webpage.
   - The src attribute specifies the image source.
   - The alt attribute provides alternative text for accessibility.
   - **Example:**

HTML

- <img src="image.jpg" alt="A beautiful landscape">
  - **Personal Insight:** Always include the alt attribute. It's not just for accessibility; it also helps if the image fails to load.

5. **Lists (<ul>, <ol>, <li>):**
   - Used to create unordered (bulleted) and ordered (numbered) lists.
   - <ul> for unordered lists, <ol> for ordered lists, and <li> for list items.
   - **Example:**

HTML

```
<ul>

<li>Item 1</li>

<li>Item 2</li>
```

```
<li>Item 3</li>
```

```
</ul>
```

```
<ol>
```

```
<li>First Step</li>
```

```
<li>Second Step</li>
```

```
<li>Third Step</li>
```

```
</ol>
```

Expert Commentary: Use lists to organize related information.

6. **Divisions and Spans (<div>, <span>):**
   - <div> is a block-level element used to group elements.
   - <span> is an inline element used to group text or inline elements.
   - **Example:**

HTML

- <div>

- <p>This is a paragraph inside a div.</p>
- <span>This is some inline text.</span>
- </div>
  - **Personal Insight:** While <div> and <span> are versatile, avoid overusing them. Prefer semantic elements when possible.

Essential HTML Attributes: The Fine Details

1. href:
   - Specifies the URL of a hyperlink.
   - Used with the <a> element.
2. src:
   - Specifies the source URL of an image or other media.
   - Used with the <img>, <video>, and <audio> elements.
3. alt:
   - Provides alternative text for an image.
   - Used with the <img> element.
4. class:
   - Specifies one or more class names for an element.
   - Used to apply CSS styles to multiple elements.
5. id:
   - Specifies a unique ID for an element.
   - Used to apply CSS styles or JavaScript behavior to a specific element.
6. style:
   - Specifies inline CSS styles for an element.
   - **Example:**

- `<p style="color: blue; font-size: 16px;">This text is styled inline.</p>`
  - **Expert Commentary:** Avoid inline styles as much as possible, use external stylesheets instead.

Practical Implementation: Step-by-Step

1. **Create a New HTML File:** Start with the basic HTML structure.
2. **Add Headings and Paragraphs:** Use `<h1>` to `<h6>` and `<p>` tags to add content.
3. **Create Links:** Use `<a>` tags to create hyperlinks.
4. **Embed Images:** Use `<img>` tags to embed images.
5. **Create Lists:** Use `<ul>` and `<ol>` tags to create lists.
6. **Use `<div>` and `<span>`:** Use `<div>` and `<span>` tags to group elements.
7. **Add Attributes:** Use attributes like href, src, alt, class, and id to add additional information.
8. **Test Your Code:** Open your HTML file in a web browser to see the results.

2.3: Forms, Tables, and Multimedia Integration

These elements add interactivity and rich content to your web pages. Let's break them down.

Forms: Gathering User Input

Forms are essential for collecting user data, like login credentials, contact information, or survey responses.

1. `<form>` **Element:**
   - Defines a form and its attributes.

- action attribute specifies the URL where the form data is sent.
- method attribute specifies the HTTP method (GET or POST).
- **Example:**

HTML

```
<form action="/submit" method="post">

</form>
```

2. **Input Elements (<input>):**
   - Used to create various input fields.
   - type attribute specifies the input type (text, password, email, etc.).
   - name attribute specifies the name of the input field.
   - **Example:**

HTML

```
<label for="username">Username:</label>

<input type="text" id="username" name="username"><br><br>

<label for="password">Password:</label>

<input type="password" id="password" name="password"><br><br>
```

```
<label for="email">Email:</label>
```

```
<input type="email" id="email" name="email"><br><br>
```

```
<input type="submit" value="Submit">
```

3. `<textarea>` **Element:**
   ○ Used to create a multi-line text input.
   ○ **Example:**

HTML

```
<label for="message">Message:</label><br>
```

```
<textarea id="message" name="message" rows="4" cols="50"></textarea><br><br>
```

4. `<select>` **and** `<option>` **Elements:**
   ○ Used to create a dropdown list.
   ○ **Example:**

HTML

```
<label for="country">Country:</label>
```

```
<select id="country" name="country">

  <option value="usa">USA</option>

  <option value="canada">Canada</option>

  <option value="uk">UK</option>

</select><br><br>
```

5. <label> **Element:**
   - Provides a label for an input element.
   - Improves accessibility and user experience.
   - Use the for attribute to associate a label with an input element.

Tables: Displaying Tabular Data

Tables are used to present data in a structured format.

1. <table> **Element:**
   - Defines a table.
2. <tr> **Element:**
   - Defines a table row.
3. <th> **Element:**
   - Defines a table header cell.
4. <td> **Element:**
   - Defines a table data cell.
   - **Example:**

HTML

```
<table>

  <tr>

    <th>Name</th>

    <th>Age</th>

    <th>City</th>

  </tr>

  <tr>

    <td>John Doe</td>

    <td>30</td>

    <td>New York</td>

  </tr>

  <tr>

    <td>Jane Smith</td>

    <td>25</td>

    <td>London</td>

  </tr>

</table>
```

Personal Insight: Resist the urge to use tables for layout. CSS is far more appropriate. Tables should be used for data.

Multimedia Integration: Adding Rich Content

1. <video> **Element:**
   - Used to embed video content.
   - src attribute specifies the video source.
   - controls attribute adds video controls.
   - **Example:**

HTML

```
<video src="video.mp4" controls width="640" height="360"></video>
```

2. <audio> **Element:**
   - Used to embed audio content.
   - src attribute specifies the audio source.
   - controls attribute adds audio controls.
   - **Example:**

HTML

```
<audio src="audio.mp3" controls></audio>
```

3. <picture> **Element:**

  ○ Used for responsive images.

  ○ Allows you to specify different image sources for different screen sizes.

  ○ **Example:**

HTML

```
<picture>

  <source srcset="large.jpg" media="(min-width: 1024px)">

  <source srcset="medium.jpg" media="(min-width: 768px)">

  <img src="small.jpg" alt="A responsive image">

</picture>
```

Expert Commentary: Optimize multimedia files for web use to improve performance. Use appropriate file formats and compress files.

Practical Implementation: Step-by-Step

1. **Create a Form:** Use the <form> element and add input elements, textareas, and select elements.
2. **Create a Table:** Use the <table>, <tr>, <th>, and <td> elements to create a table.
3. **Embed Multimedia:** Use the <video>, <audio>, and <picture> elements to embed multimedia content.
4. **Test Your Code:** Open your HTML file in a web browser to see the results.

Chapter 3: Styling with CSS

Welcome to the world of Cascading Style Sheets (CSS)! If HTML is the skeleton of your website, CSS is the wardrobe, the makeup, and the interior design. It's what makes your website visually appealing and unique.

3.1: CSS Selectors and Properties

CSS is what gives your HTML structure its style. To do this effectively, you need to understand how to select elements and apply properties.

CSS Selectors: Targeting Elements

Selectors are patterns used to select the HTML elements you want to style.

1. **Element Selectors:**
   - Selects all elements of a specific type.
   - **Example:**CSS
   - p {   color: blue;}
   - This will style all <p> elements on the page.
2. **Class Selectors:**
   - Selects elements with a specific class attribute.
   - Uses a dot (.) followed by the class name.
   - **Example:**

CSS

   - .highlight {background-color: yellow;}
   - This will style all elements with class="highlight".

3. **ID Selectors:**
    - Selects a single element with a specific ID attribute.
    - Uses a hash (#) followed by the ID name.
    - **Example:**

CSS

    - #main-title { font-size: 24px;}
    - This will style the element with id="main-title".
    - **Personal Insight:** IDs should be unique. Avoid using the same ID multiple times on a page.

4. **Attribute Selectors:**
    - Selects elements with specific attributes or attribute values.
    - **Example:**CSS
    - a[href^="https://"] { color: green;}
    - This will style all <a> elements whose href attribute starts with "https://".

5. **Combinators:**
    - Combine selectors to target specific elements based on their relationships.
    - **Descendant Combinator (space):** Selects all descendant elements.
        - div p selects all <p> elements inside <div> elements.
    - **Child Combinator (>):** Selects all direct child elements.
        - div > p selects all <p> elements that are direct children of <div> elements.
    - **Adjacent Sibling Combinator (+):** Selects the next sibling element.
        - h2 + p selects the first <p> element that comes immediately after an <h2> element.
    - **General Sibling Combinator (~):** Selects all sibling elements that follow.
        - h2 ~ p selects all <p> elements that come after an <h2> element.

6. **Pseudo-classes:**
    o Selects elements based on their state (e.g., hover, active, focus).
    o **Example:**CSS
    o a:hover {color: red;}
    o This will change the color of <a> elements when the mouse hovers over them.

CSS Properties: Applying Styles

Properties define the styles you want to apply to selected elements.

1. **Color:**
    o color: Specifies the text color.
    o background-color: Specifies the background color.
    o **Example:**

CSS

    o p { color: #333; background-color: #f0f0f0;}
2. **Typography:**
    o font-family: Specifies the font.
    o font-size: Specifies the font size.
    o font-weight: Specifies the font weight.
    o text-align: Specifies the text alignment.
    o **Example:**

- h1 { font-family: Arial, sans-serif; font-size: 32px; font-weight: bold; text-align: center;}

3. **Box Model:**
   - width: Specifies the width of an element.
   - height: Specifies the height of an element.
   - padding: Specifies the padding around the content.
   - border: Specifies the border around the padding and content.
   - margin: Specifies the margin outside the border.
   - **Example:**

- div { width: 200px; height: 100px; padding: 10px;border: 1px solid black; margin: 20px;}

4. **Display:**
   - display: Specifies the display type of an element.
   - display: block; (block-level element)
   - display: inline; (inline element)
   - display: inline-block; (inline-level block container)
   - display: flex;
   - display: grid;
   - **Personal Insight:** Understanding the display property is crucial for layout control.

Practical Implementation: Step-by-Step

1. **Create an HTML File:** Add some HTML elements to your file.
2. **Create a CSS File:** Create a separate CSS file and link it to your HTML file using the <link> tag.
3. **Use Selectors:** Use various selectors to target the HTML elements you want to style.
4. **Apply Properties:** Apply CSS properties to the selected elements to change their appearance.
5. **Test Your Code:** Open your HTML file in a web browser to see the results.

3.2: The Box Model and Layout Fundamentals

Understanding the box model and basic layout principles is essential for controlling the visual presentation of your web pages.

The Box Model: The Foundation of Layout

The CSS box model describes how HTML elements are rendered as rectangular boxes. Each box consists of four areas: content, padding, border, and margin.

1. **Content:**
   - The actual content of the element (text, images, etc.).
   - Its dimensions are determined by the content itself or by explicitly set width and height properties.
2. **Padding:**
   - The space between the content and the border.
   - Controlled by the padding property.
   - **Example:**CSS
   - div { padding: 20px; / 20px padding on all sides / padding-top: 10px; / 10px top padding / padding-right: 15px; / 15px right padding /padding-bottom:20px; / 20px bottom padding / padding-left: 25px; / 25pxleft padding /}
3. **Border:**

- o The border surrounding the padding and content.
- o Controlled by the border property.
- o **Example:**CSS
- o div { border: 2px solid black; / 2px solid black border / border-width: 1px; border-style: dashed; border-color: red;}

4. **Margin:**
   - o The space outside the border.
   - o Controlled by the margin property.
   - o **Example:**CSS
   - o div {margin: 10px; / 10px margin on all sides /margin-top: 5px; / 5px top margin /margin-right: 10px; / 10px right margin /margin-bottom: 15px; / 15px bottom margin / margin-left: 20px; / 20px left margin /}

Personal Insight: Visualizing the box model with your browser's dev tools is a fantastic way to fully grasp it. I spent a lot of time with the element inspector.

Layout Fundamentals: Organizing Content

1. **Block-Level Elements:**
   - o Start on a new line and take up the full width of their parent container.
   - o Examples: <div>, <p>, <h1> to <h6>.
2. **Inline Elements:**
   - o Flow within the text and take up only the space they need.
   - o Examples: <span>, <a>, <img>.
3. **Inline-Block Elements:**
   - o Behave like inline elements but can have width and height properties.
   - o Controlled by display: inline-block;.
4. **Display Property:**

- Controls how an element is displayed.
- display: block;: Makes an element block-level.
- display: inline;: Makes an element inline.
- display: inline-block;: Makes an element inline-block.
- display: none;: Hides an element.
- display: flex;: Enables flexbox layout.
- display: grid;: Enables grid layout.
- **Expert Commentary:** The display property is fundamental for layout control. It allows you to change the default behavior of elements.

5. **Position Property:**
   - Controls the position of an element.
   - position: static;: Default position.Elements are positioned according to the normal flow of the document.
   - position: relative;: Positions an element relative to its normal position.
   - position: absolute;: Positions an element relative to its nearest positioned ancestor.
   - position: fixed;: Positions an element relative to the viewport.
   - position: sticky;: Positions an element based on the user's scroll position.

Personal Insight: position: absolute and position: relative can be tricky, but once you understand how they work together, they're incredibly powerful.

Practical Implementation: Step-by-Step

1. **Create an HTML File:** Add some <div> elements with content.
2. **Create a CSS File:** Link it to your HTML file.
3. **Apply Box Model Properties:** Use padding, border, and margin to style the <div> elements.

4. **Experiment with Display:** Change the display property of the <div> elements to see how they behave.
5. **Experiment with Position:** Change the position property of the <div> elements to see how they behave.
6. **Test Your Code:** Open your HTML file in a web browser and inspect the elements using developer tools.

3.3: Visual Design: Text, Colors, and Backgrounds

These elements are crucial for creating a visually appealing and engaging user experience.

Text Styling: Conveying Information Clearly

1. font-family:
   - Specifies the font family to use.
   - Use a fallback font in case the primary font is not available.
   - **Example:**

CSS

```
p { font-family: 'Arial', sans-serif}
```

   - **Expert Commentary:** Choose fonts that are readable and consistent with your brand. Limit the number of font families used.
2. font-size:
   - Specifies the font size.
   - Use relative units (em, rem) for better responsiveness.

- ○ **Example:**

CSS

```
h1 {font-size: 2rem;}
```

- ○ **Personal Insight:** I used to use pixel values for font sizes, but rem units have made my life easier. They scale better with user preferences and across devices.
3. font-weight:
   - ○ Specifies the font weight (e.g., bold, normal).
   - ○ **Example:**

CSS

```
strong {font-weight: bold;}
```

4. text-align:
   - ○ Specifies the text alignment (left, right, center, justify).
   - ○ **Example:**

CSS

```css
h1 { text-align: center;}
```

5. line-height:
   - Specifies the line height.
   - Improves readability by adding space between lines.
   - **Example:**

CSS

```css
p {line-height: 1.6;}
```

6. color:
   - Specifies the text color.
   - Use hex codes, RGB, or named colors.
   - **Example:**

CSS

```css
p { color: #333;}
```

Colors: Setting the Tone

1. color:
   - Specifies the text color.
   - **Example:**CSS

```
h1 {color: #007bff; / Blue /}
```

2. background-color:
   - Specifies the background color.
   - **Example:**CSS

```
body {  background-color: #f0f0f0; / Light gray /}
```

3. **Color Formats:**
   - **Hex Codes:** #rrggbb (e.g., #ff0000 for red).
   - **RGB:** rgb(red, green, blue) (e.g., rgb(255, 0, 0) for red).
   - **RGBA:** rgba(red, green, blue, alpha) (e.g., rgba(255, 0, 0, 0.5) for semi-transparent red).
   - **HSL:** hsl(hue, saturation, lightness)
   - **HSLA:** hsla(hue, saturation, lightness, alpha)
   - **Named Colors:** (e.g., red, blue, green).
   - **Personal Insight:** RGBA and HSLA are fantastic for creating overlays and subtle color effects.

Backgrounds: Adding Visual Interest

1. background-image:
   - Specifies a background image.
   - **Example:**

CSS

body (background-image: url('background.jpg');}

2. background-repeat:
   - Controls how the background image is repeated.
   - Values: repeat, repeat-x, repeat-y, no-repeat.
   - **Example:**CSS

body {background-repeat: no-repeat;}

3. background-position:
   - Controls the position of the background image.
   - Values: top, bottom, left, right, center, or pixel/percentage values.
   - **Example:**

CSS

```css
body { background-position: center top;}
```

4. background-size:
    - Controls the size of the background image.
    - Values: auto, cover, contain, or pixel/percentage values.
    - **Example:**

CSS

```css
body {background-size: cover;}
```

5. background **(Shorthand):**
    - Sets multiple background properties in one declaration.
    - **Example:**

CSS

```css
body {background: url('background.jpg') no-repeat center top cover;}
```

Practical Implementation: Step-by-Step

1. **Create an HTML File:** Add some text elements.
2. **Create a CSS File:** Link it to your HTML file.
3. **Style Text:** Use font-family, font-size, font-weight, text-align, and line-height to style the text.
4. **Add Colors:** Use color and background-color to add colors to the text and background.

5. **Add Background Images:** Use background-image, background-repeat, background-position, and background-size to add background images.

6. **Experiment with Color Formats:** Try different color formats like hex codes, RGB, and RGBA.

7. **Test Your Code:** Open your HTML file in a web browser to see the results.

Chapter 4: Responsive Design and Layouts

In today's digital landscape, websites need to look great and function flawlessly on a wide range of devices, from desktops to smartphones. That's where responsive design comes in.

4.1: Responsive Design Principles and Techniques

In today's multi-device world, websites need to look and function flawlessly across desktops, tablets, and smartphones. Responsive design is the key to achieving this.

The Essence of Responsive Design

Responsive design is about creating websites that adapt their layout and content to different screen sizes and resolutions. It's not just about shrinking or stretching content; it's about providing an optimal user experience on every device.

Core Principles:

1. **Fluid Grids:**
   - Instead of using fixed units (pixels) for widths and heights, use relative units (percentages).
   - This allows elements to scale proportionally to their containers.
   - **Example:**

CSS

   - .container {width: 90%; / Takes up 90% of the parent container's width /max-width: 1200px; / Prevents the container from becoming too wide on large screens /margin: 0 auto; / Centers the container /}

- **Personal Insight:** Switching to percentage-based widths was a game-changer for me. It made my layouts much more flexible and adaptable.

2. **Flexible Images:**
   - Images should scale proportionally to fit their containers.
   - Use the max-width: 100%; and height: auto; properties.
   - **Example:**

CSS

- img { max-width: 100%; height: auto; display: block; / Prevents extra space below the image /}
- **Expert Commentary:** Consider using responsive image techniques like the <picture> element or srcset attribute for better performance.

3. **Media Queries:**
   - Use media queries to apply different styles based on screen size, orientation, and other device characteristics.
   - They allow you to define breakpoints and apply specific CSS rules for each breakpoint.
   - **Example:**

CSS

- @media (max-width: 768px) { / Styles for screens 768px wide or less /body { font-size: 16px; } .container { width: 100%; padding: 10px; }}@media (min-width: 1024px) { / Styles for screens 1024px wide or more / body { font-size: 18px; }}

4. **Mobile-First Approach:**
   - Design for mobile devices first, then progressively enhance for larger screens.
   - This ensures that your website provides a good experience on smaller screens.
   - **Personal Insight:** Adopting a mobile-first approach forced me to prioritize content and functionality. It also helped me create cleaner and more efficient code.
5. **Viewport Meta Tag:**
   - The viewport meta tag is essential for responsive design. It tells the browser how to control the page's dimensions and scaling.
   - **Example:**

HTML

   - `<meta name="viewport" content="width=device-width, initial-scale=1.0">`
   - Place this tag in the `<head>` section of your HTML document.
   - width=device-width sets the width of the viewport to the device's width.
   - initial-scale=1.0 sets the initial zoom level to 1.

Practical Implementation: Step-by-Step

1. **Add Viewport Meta Tag:** Add the viewport meta tag to your HTML document.
2. **Use Fluid Grids:** Use percentage-based widths and heights for your layout.
3. **Make Images Flexible:** Apply max-width: 100%; and height: auto; to your images.
4. **Implement Media Queries:** Define breakpoints and apply different CSS rules for each breakpoint.
5. **Test on Multiple Devices:** Use browser developer tools or real devices to test your website's responsiveness.

Key Techniques:

- **Breakpoints:** Define specific screen widths where your layout changes. Common breakpoints include:
  - Mobile: 320px - 480px
  - Tablet: 768px - 1024px
  - Desktop: 1024px and above
- **Flexbox and Grid:** Use Flexbox and Grid for flexible and responsive layouts.
- **Responsive Typography:** Adjust font sizes and line heights for different screen sizes.

4.2: Media Queries and Breakpoint Implementation

Media queries are the backbone of responsive design, allowing you to tailor your website's appearance based on various device characteristics. Breakpoints are the specific points at which those changes occur.

Understanding Media Queries

Media queries are CSS rules that apply styles only when certain conditions are met. These conditions can be based on screen size, orientation, resolution, and more.

1. **Syntax:**
   - Media queries are written using the @media rule.
   - **Example:**

CSS

@media (max-width: 768px) { / Styles to apply when the screen width is 768px or less /}

2. **Media Types:**
   - all: Applies to all media types.
   - screen: Applies to screens (desktops, laptops, tablets, smartphones).
   - print: Applies to printed documents.
   - **Example:**

CSS

@media screen and (max-width: 768px) {/ Styles for screens 768px wide or less /}

3. **Media Features:**
   - width: Width of the viewport.
   - height: Height of the viewport.
   - min-width: Minimum width of the viewport.
   - max-width: Maximum width of the viewport.
   - orientation: Orientation of the viewport (portrait or landscape).
   - resolution: Resolution of the viewport.
   - **Example:**

CSS

@media (min-width: 1024px) and (orientation: landscape) { / Styles for landscape screens 1024px wide or more /}

4. **Logical Operators:**
   - and: Combines multiple media features.

- not: Negates a media feature.
- only: Applies styles only if the entire query matches.
- , (comma): Acts as an "or" operator.
- **Example:**

CSS

@media not print and (max-width: 768px) { / Styles for screens 768px or less, but not for print /}

Implementing Breakpoints

Breakpoints are specific screen widths at which your website's layout changes. They allow you to define different styles for different device categories.

1. **Choosing Breakpoints:**
    - There's no one-size-fits-all approach. Consider your content and design.
    - Common breakpoints include:
        - Mobile: 320px - 480px
        - Tablet: 768px - 1024px
        - Desktop: 1024px and above
    - **Personal Insight:** I like to test on real devices to see how the layout responds. This helps me fine-tune my breakpoints.
2. **Implementation:**
    - Use media queries to apply different styles at each breakpoint.
    - **Example:**

CSS

/ Default styles /body { font-size: 16px;}

.container { width: 90%; margin: 0 auto;}/ Mobile styles /@media (max-width: 768px) { body {font-size: 14px; } .container {width: 100%; padding: 10px; } .column { width: 100%; /stack columns on mobile/ }}/ Desktop styles /@media (min-width: 1024px) { body { font-size: 18px;}}

3. **Mobile-First Approach:**
   ○ Start with styles for mobile devices and then use media queries to add styles for larger screens.
   ○ This ensures that your website provides a good experience on smaller screens.
   ○ **Expert Commentary:** Mobile-first is a best practice. It forces you to prioritize content and functionality.

Practical Implementation: Step-by-Step

1. **Identify Breakpoints:** Determine the screen widths at which you want your layout to change.
2. **Write Media Queries:** Use the @media rule to define media queries for each breakpoint.
3. **Apply Styles:** Add CSS rules inside each media query to apply different styles.
4. **Test on Multiple Devices:** Use browser developer tools or real devices to test your website's responsiveness.
5. **Refine Breakpoints:** Adjust your breakpoints and styles based on your testing results.

Key Considerations:

- **Content Prioritization:** Use breakpoints to prioritize content and functionality on different devices.
- **Layout Changes:** Use breakpoints to change the layout of your website, such as stacking columns on mobile devices.
- **Typography Adjustments:** Use breakpoints to adjust font sizes and line heights for different screen sizes.
- **Image Optimization:** Use the <picture> element or srcset attribute to provide different image sources for different screen sizes.

4.3: Flexible Layouts: Flexbox and Grid

Flexbox and Grid are powerful CSS layout modules that revolutionize how we create responsive and flexible layouts. They provide more control and flexibility than traditional layout methods.

Flexbox: One-Dimensional Layouts

Flexbox (Flexible Box Layout) is designed for one-dimensional layouts, meaning it works along a single axis (either rows or columns).

1. **Enabling Flexbox:**
   - Use display: flex; to make an element a flex container.
   - **Example:**

CSS

```
.flex-container {display: flex;}
```

2. **Flex Direction:**
   - flex-direction property defines the direction of the main axis.
   - Values: row, row-reverse, column, column-reverse.
   - **Example:**

CSS

.flex-container { flex-direction: row; / Default: items are arranged in a row /}

3. **Justify Content:**
   - justify-content property aligns items along the main axis.
   - Values: flex-start, flex-end, center, space-between, space-around, space-evenly.
   - **Example:**

CSS

.flex-container { justify-content: space-between; / Distributes items evenly with space between them /}

4. **Align Items:**
   - align-items property aligns items along the cross axis (perpendicular to the main axis).
   - Values: flex-start, flex-end, center, baseline, stretch.
   - **Example:**

CSS

.flex-container { align-items: center; / Centers items vertically /}

5. **Flex Grow, Shrink, and Basis:**
   - These properties control how flex items grow or shrink to fit the available space.[4]
   - flex-grow: Specifies how much an item will grow relative to other flex items.
   - flex-shrink: Specifies how much an item will shrink relative to other flex items.
   - flex-basis: Specifies the initial main size of a flex item.
   - **Example:**

CSS

.flex-item { flex: 1; / Shorthand for flex-grow: 1, flex-shrink: 1, flex-basis: 0 /}

   - **Personal Insight:** Flexbox changed how I built navigation bars and aligned content. It's perfect for single row or column layouts.

Grid: Two-Dimensional Layouts

Grid (CSS Grid Layout) is designed for two-dimensional layouts, allowing you to create complex grid-based layouts with rows and columns.[5]

1. **Enabling Grid:**
   - Use display: grid; to make an element a grid container.

- Example:

CSS

.grid-container {display: grid;}

2. **Grid Template Columns and Rows:**
   - grid-template-columns and grid-template-rows properties define the number and size of columns and rows.
   - Use fixed units (px), relative units (fr), or percentages.
   - **Example:**

CSS

.grid-container {grid-template-columns: 1fr 2fr 1fr; / Three columns, middle column twice as wide /grid-template-rows: auto 100px; / Two rows, second row 100px high /}

3. **Grid Gap:**
   - grid-gap property adds space between rows and columns.
   - **Example:**

CSS

.grid-container { grid-gap: 20px; / 20px gap between rows and columns /}

4. **Grid Area:**
   - grid-area property assigns a name to a grid item.
   - Use grid-template-areas to define the layout using named grid areas.
   - **Example:**

CSS

.grid-container { display: grid; grid-template-areas: "header header header""main main aside""footer footer footer";}.header { grid-area: header;}.main {grid-area: main;}.aside {grid-area: aside;}.footer { grid-area: footer;}

5. **Grid Item Placement:**
   - grid-column and grid-row properties place grid items in specific grid cells.
   - **Example:**

CSS

.grid-item {grid-column: 2 / 4; / Spans from column line 2 to 4 /grid-row: 1 / 3; / Spans from row line 1 to 3 /}

- ○ **Expert Commentary:** Grid is ideal for complex layouts, such as magazine-style layouts or dashboards. It gives you precise control over the placement of elements.

Practical Implementation: Step-by-Step

1. **Create an HTML File:** Add some <div> elements to your file.
2. **Create a CSS File:** Link it to your HTML file.
3. **Implement Flexbox:** Use display: flex; and other flexbox properties to create a flexible layout.
4. **Implement Grid:** Use display: grid; and other grid properties to create a grid-based layout.
5. **Test on Multiple Devices:** Use browser developer tools or real devices to test your layouts.

Choosing Between Flexbox and Grid:

- **Flexbox:** Use for one-dimensional layouts (rows or columns).[7]
- **Grid:** Use for two-dimensional layouts (rows and columns).

Chapter 5: Enhancing Interactivity with JavaScript

If HTML provides the structure and CSS the style, JavaScript brings the interactivity. It's the language that makes your web pages dynamic and responsive to user actions.

5.1: JavaScript Basics: Variables, Functions, DOM

JavaScript is the language that brings interactivity to web pages. Let's start with the essential building blocks.

Variables: Storing Data

Variables are used to store and manipulate data in JavaScript.

1. **Declaration:**
   - Use let, const, or var to declare variables.
   - let and const are preferred over var in modern JavaScript.
   - let allows you to reassign values, while const creates constants (values that cannot be reassigned).
   - **Example:**

JavaScript

   - let name = "John Doe";
   - const age = 30;
   - let isStudent = true;

2. **Data Types:**

- JavaScript has several data types, including:
  - **String:** Text enclosed in quotes (e.g., "Hello").
  - **Number:** Numeric values (e.g., 10, 3.14).
  - **Boolean:** True or false values.
  - **Undefined:** A variable that has been declared but not assigned a value.
  - **Null:** A deliberate assignment of no value.
  - **Object:** A collection of key-value pairs.
  - **Array:** An ordered list of values.
- **Example:**

JavaScript

```
let message = "Welcome!";
let count = 10;
let isActive = false;
let person = { name: "Jane", age: 25 };
let numbers = [1, 2, 3];
```

- I remember the confusion with var, let, and const. Using let and const consistently makes your code much cleaner and easier to understand, especially when dealing with scope.

Functions: Reusable Code Blocks

Functions are blocks of code that perform specific tasks.

1. **Function Declaration:**
   - Use the function keyword to declare a function.
   - **Example:**

JavaScript

- function greet(name) { console.log("Hello, " + name + "!");}greet("Alice");
  //Output: Hello, Alice!

2. **Function Expressions:**
   - Assign a function to a variable.
   - **Example:**

JavaScript

- const greet = function(name) {console.log("Hello, " + name + "!");};
- greet("Bob"); // Output: Hello, Bob!

3. **Arrow Functions:**
   - A more concise syntax for writing functions.
   - **Example:**

JavaScript

- const greet = (name) => { console.log("Hello, " + name + "!");};greet("Charlie");
  // Output: Hello, Charlie!

4. **Return Values:**
   - Functions can return values using the return keyword.
   - **Example:**

JavaScript

- function add(a, b) {return a + b;}let sum = add(5, 3); // sum = 8
- **Expert Commentary:** Functions are essential for organizing your code and making it reusable. Use them to break down complex tasks into smaller, manageable pieces.

DOM: Interacting with the HTML Structure

The Document Object Model (DOM) is a programming interface for HTML and XML documents. It represents the page as a tree-like structure, allowing JavaScript to access and manipulate elements.

1. **Accessing Elements:**
   - Use methods like document.getElementById(), document.querySelector(), and document.querySelectorAll() to access elements.
   - **Example:**

JavaScript

- const title = document.getElementById("main-title");
- const paragraphs = document.querySelectorAll("p");
- const firstParagraph = document.querySelector("p");

2. **Manipulating Elements:**
   - Use properties like innerHTML, textContent, and style to modify elements.
   - **Example:**

JavaScript

- ○ title.textContent = "New Title";
- ○ paragraphs[0].style.color = "red";

3. **Creating Elements:**
   - ○ Use document.createElement() to create new elements.
   - ○ Use appendChild() to add elements to the DOM.
   - ○ **Example:**

const newParagraph = document.createElement("p");

newParagraph.textContent = "This is a new paragraph.";

document.body.appendChild(newParagraph);1

The DOM can seem intimidating at first, but it's incredibly powerful. Once you understand the tree structure, you can manipulate any element on the page.

Practical Implementation: Step-by-Step

1. **Create an HTML File:** Add some HTML elements with IDs and classes.
2. **Create a JavaScript File:** Link it to your HTML file using the <script> tag.
3. **Declare Variables:** Use let and const to declare variables.
4. **Create Functions:** Use function or arrow functions to create functions.
5. **Access DOM Elements:** Use document.getElementById(), document.querySelector(), or document.querySelectorAll() to access elements.
6. **Manipulate Elements:** Use properties like textContent and style to modify elements.

7. **Create New Elements:** Use document.createElement() and appendChild() to create and add new elements.

8. **Test Your Code:** Open your HTML file in a web browser and use the browser's developer console to check the results.

5.2: Event Handling and Dynamic Content

Event handling and dynamic content are what make your websites interactive and engaging. They allow users to interact with elements and see immediate changes.

Event Handling: Responding to User Interactions

Event handling is the process of responding to user actions, such as clicks, mouseovers, and key presses.

1. **Event Listeners:**
   - The addEventListener() method is used to attach an event listener to an element.
   - It takes two arguments: the event type and the callback function.
   - **Example:**

```
const button = document.getElementById("myButton");
button.addEventListener("click", function() {
console.log("Button clicked!");1
});
```

2. **Event Types:**
   - Mouse Events: click, mouseover, mouseout, mousedown, mouseup, mousemove.
   - Keyboard Events: keydown, keyup, keypress.
   - Form Events: submit, change, focus, blur.
   - Window Events: load, resize, scroll.
   - **Example:**

JavaScript

```
const input = document.getElementById("myInput");
input.addEventListener("change", function() {
   console.log("Input value changed:", input.value);});
```

3. **Event Object:**
   - The event object contains information about the event.
   - It's passed as an argument to the callback function.
   - Example:

JavaScript

```
button.addEventListener("click", function(event) {
    console.log("Event type:", event.type);
    console.log("Target element:", event.target)});
```

4. **Prevent Default Behavior:**
    o The preventDefault() method prevents the default behavior of an event.
    o **Example:**

JavaScript

```
const link = document.getElementById("myLink");

link.addEventListener("click", function(event) { event.preventDefault(); // Prevents the link
from navigating

    console.log("Link clicked, but navigation prevented.");});
```

preventDefault() is crucial for form validation and custom link behavior. It gives you control over how events are handled.
Dynamic Content: Updating the Page in Real Time
Dynamic content refers to updating the content of a web page without reloading it.

1. **Manipulating DOM Elements:**
    o Use properties like innerHTML, textContent, and style to modify elements.
    o **Example:**
JavaScript
```
const message = document.getElementById("message");

message.textContent = "New message!";

message.style.color = "blue";
```

2. Creating and Appending Elements:

- o Use document.createElement() to create new elements.
- o Use appendChild() to add elements to the DOM.
- o **Example**:

JavaScript

```
const newParagraph = document.createElement("p");

newParagraph.textContent = "This is a dynamically created paragraph.";

document.body.appendChild(newParagraph);
```

3. **Updating Content Based on User Input:**
   - o Use event listeners to update content based on user actions.
   - o **Example:**

JavaScript

```
const input = document.getElementById("userInput");

const output = document.getElementById("output");

input.addEventListener("input", function() { output.textContent = input.value;});
```

4. **Using Timers**:
   - o Use setTimeout() and setInterval() to execute code after a delay or at regular intervals.
   - o Example:

JavaScript

```
setTimeout(function() {

  console.log("This message appears after 2 seconds.");}, 2000);let count = 0;

const interval = setInterval(function() {
```

```
count++;

console.log("Count:", count);

if (count >= 5) {

clearInterval(interval);  }}, 1000);
```

- Expert Commentary: Timers are useful for animations, delays, and periodic updates. But be mindful of performance and clear intervals when they are no longer needed.

Practical Implementation: Step-by-Step

1. Create an HTML File: Add elements with IDs to your file.
2. Create a JavaScript File: Link it to your HTML file.
3. Add Event Listeners: Use addEventListener() to attach event listeners to the elements.
4. Write Callback Functions: Write functions to handle the events.
5. Manipulate DOM Elements: Use DOM manipulation methods to update content.
6. Use Timers (Optional): Use setTimeout() or setInterval() to add timed functionality.
7. Test Your Code: Open your HTML file in a web browser and test the interactivity.

5.3: Interactive UI Elements: Modals, Sliders, etc.

Interactive UI elements like modals and sliders enhance user engagement and provide a more dynamic experience.

Modals: Pop-Up Windows

Modals are pop-up windows that display content or require user interaction.[1]

1. **HTML Structure:**
   - Create a <div> element for the modal and another for the modal content.
   - Add a button to open the modal and a close button inside the modal.
   - **Example:**

HTML

```
<button id="openModal">Open Modal</button>

<div id="myModal" class="modal">

  <div class="modal-content">

    <span class="close">&times;</span>

    <p>This is the modal content.</p>

  </div>

</div>
```

2. **CSS Styling:**
   - Style the modal to position it in the center of the screen and hide it initially.
   - **Example:**

CSS

```
.modal {

  display: none; / Hidden by default /

  position: fixed; / Stay in place /

  z-index: 1; / Sit on top /

  left: 0;
```

```
    top: 0;

    width: 100%; / Full width /

    height: 100%; / Full height /

    overflow: auto; / Enable scroll if needed /

    background-color: rgba(0, 0, 0, 0.4); / Black w/ opacity /}
.modal-content {background-color: #fefefe;

    margin: 15% auto; / 15% from the top and centered /

    padding: 20px;

    border: 1px solid #888;

    width: 80%; / Could be more or less, depending on screen size /}


.close { color: #aaa;

    float: right;

    font-size: 28px;

    font-weight: bold;}
.close:hover,

.close:focus { color: black;

    text-decoration: none;

    cursor: pointer;}
```

3. **JavaScript Functionality:**

- Add event listeners to the open and close buttons.
- Toggle the modal's display property to show or hide it.
- **Example:**

JavaScript

```javascript
const modal = document.getElementById("myModal");

const btn = document.getElementById("openModal");

const span = document.getElementsByClassName("close")[0];


btn.onclick = function() {

  modal.style.display = "block";}


span.onclick = function() {

  modal.style.display = "none";}

window.onclick = function(event) {

  if (event.target == modal) {

    modal.style.display = "none"; }}
```

Modals are great for important messages or forms. But don't overuse them! Too many modals can be disruptive to the user experience.

Sliders/Carousels: Displaying Content Sequentially

Sliders or carousels are used to display multiple images or content items in a rotating manner.

1. **HTML Structure:**
   - Create a container for the slider and add the content items inside.
   - Add navigation buttons (optional).
   - **Example:**

HTML

```
<div class="slider">

  <div class="slide">

    <img src="image1.jpg" alt="Image 1">

  </div>

  <div class="slide">

    <img src="image2.jpg" alt="Image 2">

  </div>

  <div class="slide">

    <img src="image3.jpg" alt="Image 3">

  </div>

  <button class="prev">Previous</button>
```

```
<button class="next">Next</button>
```

```
</div>
```

2. **CSS Styling:**
    - Style the slider container and slides to create the desired layout.
    - **Example:**

CSS

```css
.slider { position: relative;

    width: 600px;

    overflow: hidden;}
.slide { display: none;

    width: 100%;}
.slide img { width: 100%;}
.prev, .next {

    position: absolute;

    top: 50%;

    transform: translateY(-50%);

    background-color: rgba(0, 0, 0, 0.5);

    color: white;
```

padding: 10px;

border: none;

cursor: pointer;}

.prev {   left: 0;}

.next {   right: 0;}

3. **JavaScript Functionality:**
   - Add event listeners to the navigation buttons.
   - Use a counter to track the current slide and update the display.
   - **Example:**

JavaScript

```
const slides = document.querySelectorAll(".slide");

const prevBtn = document.querySelector(".prev");

const nextBtn = document.querySelector(".next");

let currentSlide = 0;

function showSlide(index) { slides.forEach((slide, i) => {slide.style.display = i === index ?
"block" : "none";

    });}

function nextSlide() { currentSlide = (currentSlide + 1) % slides.length;

    showSlide(currentSlide);}
```

```
function prevSlide() { currentSlide = (currentSlide - 1 + slides.length) % slides.length;

  showSlide(currentSlide);}

nextBtn.onclick = nextSlide;

prevBtn.onclick = prevSlide;



showSlide(currentSlide); // Show the first slide initially
```

○ **Expert Commentary:** Sliders can add visual appeal, but they can also slow down your website. Optimize images and consider using CSS transitions for smoother animations.

Practical Implementation: Step-by-Step

1. **Create HTML Structures:** Add the necessary HTML elements for modals and sliders.
2. **Style with CSS:** Apply CSS styles to position and style the elements.
3. **Add JavaScript Functionality:** Use JavaScript to add interactivity and control the elements.
4. **Test Your Code:** Open your HTML file in a web browser and test the functionality.

Chapter 6: The Modern Web Design Workflow

We've covered the core technologies and interactivity; now, let's focus on the process. A solid workflow is essential for creating successful and user-friendly websites.

6.1: User-Centered Design: Research and Planning

User-centered design (UCD) is a philosophy that puts the user at the forefront of every design decision. It's about building websites that are not only visually appealing but also meet the needs and expectations of the people who will be using them.

The Foundation: Understanding Your Users

1. **User Research:**
   - The first step is to gather information about your target audience.
   - **Methods:**
     - **Surveys:** Collect quantitative data about user demographics, preferences, and behaviors.
     - **Interviews:** Gather qualitative data through one-on-one conversations with users.
     - **Usability Testing:** Observe users as they interact with your website or prototype.
     - **Analytics:** Analyze website traffic and user behavior data.
     - **Competitor Analysis:** Research your competitors' websites to identify best practices and potential areas for improvement.
   - **Example (Survey):**
     - Use tools like Google Forms or SurveyMonkey to create surveys.
     - Ask questions like:
       - "What are your primary goals when visiting this website?"
       - "What are your biggest frustrations with similar websites?"
       - "What features would you find most useful?"

- **Personal Insight:** I used to rely on my own assumptions about what users wanted. But user research taught me that I don't always know best. Real user feedback is invaluable.

2. **User Personas:**
   - Create fictional representations of your target users based on your research.
   - Personas include demographic information, goals, needs, and behaviors.
   - **Example:**
     - **Name:** Sarah Jones
     - **Age:** 28
     - **Occupation:** Marketing Manager
     - **Goals:** Find relevant industry news and connect with other professionals.
     - **Needs:** Easy navigation, clear content, mobile-friendly design.
     - **Behaviors:** Uses social media for networking, prefers concise content.

Personas help you empathize with your users and make design decisions that are aligned with their needs.

Planning: Defining the Project Scope

1. **Define Project Goals:**
   - What do you want to achieve with this website?
   - Align your goals with the needs of your users.
   - **Example:**
     - Increase website traffic by 20%.
     - Improve user engagement by 15%.
     - Generate 100 new leads per month.

2. **Create a Sitemap:**
   - Visualize the website's structure and navigation.
   - Helps you organize content and plan the user journey.
   - **Example:**
     - Home
     - About
     - Services
       - Service 1
       - Service 2
       - Service 3
     - Portfolio
     - Contact

3. **Plan Content Strategy:**
   - Determine the type and format of content for each page.
   - Consider the user's needs and goals when planning content.
   - **Example:**
     - Use clear and concise language.
     - Incorporate relevant images and videos.
     - Provide calls to action to guide users.

4. **Information Architecture (IA):**
   - Organize and structure content in a logical and intuitive way.
   - Focus on making information easy to find and understand.
   - **Example:**
     - Use clear and consistent navigation menus.
     - Group related content together.
     - Use headings and subheadings to break up text.

Practical Implementation: Step-by-Step

1. **Conduct User Research:** Choose appropriate research methods and gather data.
2. **Create User Personas:** Develop fictional representations of your target users.
3. **Define Project Goals:** Clearly outline what you want to achieve with the website.
4. **Create a Sitemap:** Map out the website's structure and navigation.
5. **Plan Content Strategy:** Determine the type and format of content for each page.
6. **Develop Information Architecture:** Organize and structure content for easy navigation.
7. **Document Your Findings:** Create a project brief or documentation to guide the design process.

Key Considerations:

- **Iterative Process:** UCD is an iterative process.Continuously gather user feedback and refine your design.
- **Collaboration:** Involve stakeholders and users throughout the design process.
- **Accessibility:** Design for users with disabilities.
- **Usability:** Ensure the website is easy to use and navigate.

6.2: Wireframing, Prototyping, and Iteration

Once you've conducted user research and planned your project, it's time to visualize your website's design. This is where wireframing, prototyping, and iteration come into play.

Wireframing: The Blueprint

Wireframes are low-fidelity representations of your website's layout. They focus on structure, content, and functionality, without getting bogged down in visual details.

1. **Purpose:**
   - To define the layout and content hierarchy of each page.

- To identify potential usability issues early in the design process.
- To facilitate communication with stakeholders.

2. **Tools:**
   - **Paper and Pencil:** Simple and quick for initial sketches.
   - **Digital Tools:** Balsamiq, Figma, Adobe XD, Sketch.
   - **Example (Balsamiq):**
     - Use basic shapes and placeholders to represent content elements.
     - Focus on layout and information flow.
     - **Personal Insight:** I find that starting with paper sketches helps me quickly explore different layout ideas before moving to digital tools.

3. **Key Elements:**
   - **Content Blocks:** Represent different sections of the page.
   - **Navigation:** Show the placement of menus and links.
   - **Forms:** Indicate input fields and buttons.
   - **Images and Media:** Use placeholders to represent images and videos.
   - **Annotations:** Add notes to explain design decisions and functionality.

Wireframes should be simple and clear. Avoid adding unnecessary details that can distract from the core functionality.

Prototyping: Bringing the Design to Life

Prototypes are high-fidelity representations of your website that simulate the user experience. They include visual design elements and interactive features.

1. **Purpose:**
   - To test the user interface and interaction design.
   - To gather user feedback on the overall experience.
   - To demonstrate the functionality of the website.

2. **Tools:**
   - **Figma, Adobe XD, Sketch:** These tools allow you to create interactive prototypes with transitions and animations.
   - **InVision, Proto.io:** Dedicated prototyping tools with advanced features.
   - **Example (Figma):**
     - Add visual design elements like colors, typography, and images.
     - Create interactive elements like buttons and forms.
     - Use transitions and animations to simulate user interactions.
     - **Personal Insight:** Prototyping is invaluable for testing usability.I've often discovered unexpected issues by watching users interact with my prototypes.

3. **Types of Prototypes:**
   - **Low-Fidelity Prototypes:** Basic and quick to create, focusing on functionality.
   - **High-Fidelity Prototypes:** Detailed and visually appealing, simulating the final product.
   - **Interactive Prototypes:** Allow users to interact with elements and navigate through the website.

Iteration: Refining the Design

Iteration is the process of continuously refining your design based on feedback and testing.

1. **Gather Feedback:**
   - Conduct usability testing with real users.
   - Collect feedback from stakeholders and team members.
   - Analyze website analytics and user behavior data.

2. **Analyze Feedback:**
   - Identify patterns and common issues.
   - Prioritize feedback based on impact and feasibility.

3. **Implement Changes:**

- Revise wireframes and prototypes based on feedback.
- Make necessary changes to the design and functionality.

4. **Repeat the Process:**
   - Continue to gather feedback and iterate on your design.
   - Design is an ongoing process.

Practical Implementation: Step-by-Step

1. **Create Wireframes:** Use your chosen tool to create wireframes for each page.
2. **Develop Prototypes:** Create high-fidelity prototypes based on your wireframes.
3. **Conduct Usability Testing:** Observe users as they interact with your prototypes.
4. **Gather Feedback:** Collect feedback from users and stakeholders.
5. **Analyze Feedback:** Identify patterns and prioritize issues.
6. **Implement Changes:** Revise your designs based on feedback.
7. **Repeat:** Continue to iterate on your design until you achieve your goals.

Key Considerations:

- **Focus on User Needs:** Always keep the user's needs and goals in mind.
- **Test Early and Often:** Gather feedback throughout the design process.
- **Be Flexible:** Be prepared to make changes based on feedback.
- **Document Your Process:** Keep track of your design decisions and iterations.

6.3: Accessibility and Performance Optimization

These are critical aspects of modern web development. Accessibility ensures your website is usable by everyone, including people with disabilities, while performance optimization ensures a smooth and fast user experience.

Accessibility: Design for Everyone

Accessibility is about making your website usable by people with disabilities. It's not just a nice-to-have; it's a fundamental requirement.

1. **Semantic HTML:**
   - Use HTML elements that accurately describe the meaning of your content.
   - This helps screen readers and assistive technologies understand the structure and content of your page.
   - **Example:**
     - Use <nav> for navigation menus, <article> for articles, and <aside> for side content.
     - **Personal Insight:** Learning semantic HTML was a turning point. It made my code more organized and accessible.
2. **ARIA Attributes:**
   - Accessible Rich Internet Applications (ARIA) attributes provide additional information to assistive technologies.
   - Use them to enhance the accessibility of dynamic content and complex UI elements.
   - **Example:**
     - aria-label, aria-describedby, aria-hidden, aria-live.
     - role="button" on elements that function as buttons.
   - **Expert Commentary:** Use ARIA attributes judiciously. Overusing them can actually hinder accessibility.
3. **Keyboard Navigation:**
   - Ensure your website is navigable using the keyboard alone.

- Use proper focus indicators and logical tab order.
- **Example:**
  - Test your website using only the keyboard.
  - Ensure all interactive elements are reachable using the tab key.

4. **Color Contrast:**
   - Ensure sufficient color contrast between text and background.
   - Use tools like WebAIM's Contrast Checker to verify contrast ratios.
   - **Example:**
     - Avoid light text on light backgrounds or dark text on dark backgrounds.

5. **Alternative Text for Images:**
   - Provide descriptive alternative text for images using the alt attribute.
   - This helps screen readers describe images to users.
   - **Example:**
     - `<img src="sunset.jpg" alt="A vibrant sunset over the ocean">`

6. **Video and Audio Accessibility:**
   - Provide captions and transcripts for video and audio content.
   - Use the `<track>` element for captions.
   - **Example:**
     - `<video src="video.mp4" controls><track src="captions.vtt" kind="captions" srclang="en"></video>`

Performance Optimization: Speed Matters

Performance optimization is about making your website load quickly and run smoothly. It directly impacts user experience and SEO.

1. **Image Optimization:**
   - Use optimized image formats (WebP, JPEG, PNG).
   - Compress images using tools like TinyPNG or ImageOptim.
   - Use responsive images (<picture> element or srcset attribute).
   - **Personal Insight:** Optimizing images can dramatically reduce page load times. I've seen sites go from seconds to milliseconds just by compressing images.

2. **Minification and Compression:**
   - Minify CSS and JavaScript files to remove unnecessary characters.
   - Compress files using Gzip or Brotli compression.
   - **Example:**
     - Use tools like UglifyJS or CSSNano for minification.
     - Configure your server to enable compression.

3. **Browser Caching:**
   - Leverage browser caching to store static assets (images, CSS, JavaScript) in the user's browser.
   - This reduces the number of server requests on subsequent visits.
   - **Example:**
     - Configure your server to set appropriate cache headers.

4. **Content Delivery Network (CDN):**
   - Use a CDN to distribute your website's assets across multiple servers.
   - This reduces latency and improves loading times for users around the world.
   - **Example:**
     - Cloudflare, Amazon CloudFront, or Google Cloud CDN.

5. **Lazy Loading:**
   - Load images and other assets only when they are visible in the viewport.
   - This improves initial page load times.

- Example:
  - Use the loading="lazy" attribute on <img> elements.

6. **Performance Testing:**
   - Use tools like Google PageSpeed Insights, Lighthouse, or WebPageTest to analyze website performance.
   - Identify and fix performance bottlenecks.
   - **Expert Commentary:** Regularly testing and monitoring website performance is crucial. It helps you identify and address issues before they impact users.

Practical Implementation: Step-by-Step

1. **Accessibility Audit:** Use accessibility tools and manual testing to identify accessibility issues.
2. **Implement Semantic HTML:** Use appropriate HTML elements to structure your content.
3. **Add ARIA Attributes:** Enhance accessibility with ARIA attributes.
4. **Optimize Images:** Compress and resize images for web use.
5. **Minify and Compress Files:** Reduce file sizes for faster loading.
6. **Enable Browser Caching:** Configure your server to leverage browser caching.
7. **Use a CDN (Optional):** Distribute your assets across a CDN.
8. **Test Performance:** Use performance testing tools to analyze and optimize your website.

Chapter 7: Advanced CSS and JavaScript Techniques

We've covered the fundamentals; now, let's explore some advanced techniques that will take your web development skills to the next level.

7.1: CSS Preprocessors and Animations

CSS preprocessors and animations are powerful tools that can streamline your workflow and add visual flair to your websites.

CSS Preprocessors: Supercharging Your CSS

CSS preprocessors like Sass and Less extend the capabilities of CSS, making it more maintainable and efficient.

1. **Variables:**
   - Store values in variables for reuse and consistency.
   - **Example (Sass):**

SCSS

   - $primary-color: #007bff;
   - .button { background-color: $primary-color; color: white;}.header {background-color: $primary-color;}
   - **Personal Insight:** Variables have saved me countless hours of searching and replacing. It's especially useful for color palettes.

2. **Nesting:**
   - Nest CSS rules to create a clear and organized hierarchy.[3]
   - **Example (Sass):**

SCSS

   - nav {
   - ul { list-style: none; li { display: inline-block; a {text-decoration: none;color: black; }

3. **Mixins:**
   - Create reusable blocks of CSS code.
   - **Example (Sass):**

SCSS

   - @mixin border-radius($radius) {
   - -webkit-border-radius: $radius;
   - -moz-border-radius: $radius;
   - border-radius: $radius;}
   - .button { @include border-radius(5px);}

4. **Functions:**
   - Perform calculations and manipulate values.
   - **Example (Sass):**

SCSS

- ○ $base-font-size: 16px;
- ○ p { font-size: $base-font-size 1.2;}

5. **Partials and Imports:**
   - ○ Split your CSS into multiple files and import them into a main file.
   - ○ **Example (Sass):**

SCSS

- ○ // _variables.scss
- ○ $primary-color: #007bff;// main.scss
- ○ @import "variables";.button { background-color: $primary-color;}

Preprocessors are invaluable for large projects. They improve code organization and maintainability.

CSS Animations: Bringing Elements to Life

CSS animations allow you to create smooth transitions and animations without JavaScript.

1. @keyframes **Rule:**
   - ○ Defines the animation sequence.
   - ○ **Example:**

CSS

- @keyframes fadeIn { from {opacity: 0; } to { opacity: 1; }}

2. animation **Property:**

- Applies the animation to an element.
- **Example:**

CSS

- .fade-in { animation: fadeIn 1s ease-in-out;}

3. **Animation Properties:**

- animation-name: Specifies the name of the @keyframes rule.
- animation-duration: Specifies the duration of the animation.
- animation-timing-function: Specifies the speed curve of the animation (e.g., ease, linear, ease-in-out).
- animation-delay: Specifies a delay before the animation starts.
- animation-iteration-count: Specifies the number of times the animation should play (e.g., infinite).
- animation-direction: Specifies whether the animation should play forwards, backwards, or alternate.
- animation-fill-mode: Specifies how the animation should apply styles before and after it plays.

CSS animations are great for subtle effects.But don't overdo it. Too many animations can be distracting.

4. **Transitions:**
   - Create smooth transitions between CSS property changes.
   - **Example:**

CSS

   - .button { background-color: #007bff; transition: background-color 0.3s ease;}.button:hover { background-color: #0056b3;}

Practical Implementation: Step-by-Step

1. **Set Up a Preprocessor (Sass/Less):** Install a preprocessor and configure your development environment.[6]
2. **Create Sass/Less Files:** Create .scss or .less files and write your CSS using preprocessor features.
3. **Compile to CSS:** Compile your preprocessor files to CSS using a compiler.
4. **Create Keyframe Animations:** Use the @keyframes rule to define animation sequences.
5. **Apply Animations:** Use the animation property to apply animations to elements.
6. **Use Transitions:** Add transitions to elements for smooth property changes.
7. **Test Your Code:** Open your HTML file in a web browser and test the animations and transitions.

7.2: Advanced JavaScript: Asynchronous Operations

Asynchronous operations are crucial for building responsive and efficient web applications.They allow JavaScript to perform tasks in the background without blocking the main thread.

Understanding Asynchronous Operations

JavaScript is single-threaded, meaning it executes code line by line. However, some operations, like fetching data from an API or handling timers, can take time. Asynchronous operations allow these tasks to run in the background, so the main thread can continue executing other code.

1. **Callbacks:**
   - Callbacks are functions that are passed as arguments to other functions and executed when an asynchronous operation completes.
   - **Example:**

JavaScript

```
function fetchData(callback) {setTimeout(function() {const data = { message:
"Data fetched!" };  callback(data); }, 1000);}fetchData(function(result) {
console.log(result.message); // Output: Data fetched!});console.log("Fetching
data..."); // This runs immediately
```

Callbacks can lead to "callback hell" (nested callbacks), making code difficult to read and maintain. That's where promises and async/await come in.

2. **Promises:**
   - Promises represent the eventual completion (or failure) of an asynchronous operation.
   - They have three states: pending, fulfilled, or rejected.
   - **Example:**

JavaScript

- ○ function fetchData() { return new Promise(function(resolve, reject) { setTimeout(function() { const data = { message: "Data fetched!" };resolve(data); }, 1000); });}fetchData() .then(function(result) { console.log(result.message); // Output: Data fetched! }) .catch(function(error) {console.error("Error:", error);});console.log("Fetching data..."); // This runs immediately
- ○ **Expert Commentary:** Promises provide a cleaner and more structured way to handle asynchronous operations. They allow you to chain multiple asynchronous tasks together.

3. **Async/Await:**
   - ○ Async/await is a more concise and readable syntax for working with promises.
   - ○ It allows you to write asynchronous code that looks like synchronous code.[12]
   - ○ **Example:**

JavaScript

- ○ async function fetchData() {try { const result = await new Promise(resolve => { setTimeout(() => {resolve({ message: "Data fetched!" }); }, 1000); }); console.log(result.message); // Output: Data fetched!} catch (error) { console.error("Error:", error); }}fetchData();console.log("Fetching data..."); // This runs immediately
- ○ **Personal Insight:** Async/await has made my asynchronous code much more readable and maintainable[3] It's my preferred way to handle asynchronous operations.

4. **Fetching Data with** fetch():
   - ○ The fetch() API is used to make network requests.

- It returns a promise that resolves with the response.
- **Example:**

JavaScript

- async function fetchData() try { const response = await fetch("https://api.example.com/data"); const data = await response.json(); console.log(data); } catch (error) {console.error("Error:", error); }}fetchData();

5. **Error Handling:**
   - Use try...catch blocks to handle errors in asynchronous code.
   - **Example:**

JavaScript

- async function fetchData() { try { const response = await fetch("https://api.example.com/data"); if (!response.ok) { throw new Error("Network response was not ok");} const data = await response.json(); console.log(data);} catch (error) { console.error("Error:", error);}}fetchData();

Practical Implementation: Step-by-Step

1. **Create an HTML File:** Add a button to trigger the asynchronous operation.
2. **Create a JavaScript File:** Link it to your HTML file.

3. **Implement Asynchronous Code:** Use callbacks, promises, or async/await to perform asynchronous tasks.[14]

4. **Fetch Data:** Use the fetch() API to make network requests.

5. **Handle Errors:** Use try...catch blocks to handle errors.

6. **Update the DOM:** Use DOM manipulation to display the results of the asynchronous operation.

7. **Test Your Code:** Open your HTML file in a web browser and test the functionality.

7.3: Introduction to Frameworks (Optional Overview)

JavaScript frameworks provide a structure for building complex web applications. They offer features like component-based architecture, state management, and routing, making development faster and more efficient.

Why Use Frameworks?

- **Component-Based Architecture:**
  - Break down your application into reusable components.
  - This promotes code reusability and maintainability.
- **State Management:**
  - Manage the application's data and state in a predictable and organized way.
  - This makes it easier to handle complex data flows.
- **Routing:**
  - Handle navigation between different views or pages in a single-page application (SPA).
- **Developer Productivity:**
  - Frameworks provide a set of tools and conventions that streamline the development process.
  - This allows you to focus on building features rather than writing boilerplate code.

Popular JavaScript Frameworks

1. **React:**
   - A JavaScript library for building user interfaces.
   - Developed by Facebook.
   - Uses a component-based architecture and a virtual DOM for efficient updates.
   - Popular for building complex SPAs.
   - **Personal Insight:** React's component-based approach changed how I think about building UIs. It's great for breaking down complex interfaces into manageable pieces.

2. **Vue.js:**
   - A progressive JavaScript framework for building user interfaces.
   - Known for its simplicity and ease of learning.
   - Uses a component-based architecture and a virtual DOM.
   - Popular for building SPAs and progressive web apps (PWAs).
   - **Expert Commentary:** Vue.js is a great choice for beginners due to its gentle learning curve and clear documentation.

3. **Angular:**
   - A full-fledged JavaScript framework developed by Google.
   - Uses TypeScript and a component-based architecture.
   - Provides a comprehensive set of tools and features for building complex applications.
   - Popular for enterprise-level applications.
   - **Personal Insight:** Angular provides a very structured project structure, which is great for large teams, but it does have a steeper learning curve.

Key Concepts Across Frameworks

- **Components:**
  - Reusable building blocks of the UI.
  - Encapsulate markup, logic, and styling.
- **State:**
  - Data that represents the current state of the application.
  - Changes in state trigger UI updates.
- **Props (Properties):**
  - Data passed from parent components to child components.
- **Events:**
  - Actions that occur in the UI, such as clicks and form submissions.
- **Routing:**
  - Handling navigation between different views or pages.
- **Virtual DOM:**
  - An in-memory representation of the DOM that allows for efficient updates.

Getting Started with a Framework

1. **Choose a Framework:**
   - Consider your project's requirements and your experience level.
2. **Set Up a Development Environment:**
   - Install Node.js and npm (Node Package Manager).
   - Use a command-line tool (e.g., Create React App, Vue CLI, Angular CLI) to create a new project.
3. **Learn the Basics:**
   - Study the framework's documentation and tutorials.
   - Start with simple projects to get familiar with the core concepts.

4. **Build Components:**

   o   Break down your UI into reusable components.

5. **Manage State:**

   o   Learn how to manage the application's data and state.

6. **Implement Routing:**

   o   Set up navigation between different views or pages.

7. **Test and Debug:**

   o   Use the framework's development tools to test and debug your application.

Practical Considerations

- **Learning Curve:** Frameworks have a learning curve. Start with the basics and gradually learn more advanced concepts.

- **Community Support:** Choose frameworks with a strong community for support and resources.

- **Project Requirements:** Consider your project's requirements when choosing a framework.

- **Personal Preference:** Choose a framework that you enjoy working with.

Chapter 8: Practical Application: Building a Website

It's time to roll up our sleeves and build a real website! This chapter will guide you through the process, from planning to deployment.

8.1: Project Planning and Structure

Before diving into code, a solid plan is essential. It's like having a blueprint before building a house. Let's break down how to plan and structure your web development project.

Defining the Project Scope

1. **Project Goals and Objectives:**
   - What are you trying to achieve? Is it a portfolio site, an e-commerce platform, or a blog?
   - Define specific, measurable, achievable, relevant, and time-bound (SMART) goals.
   - **Example:**
     - Goal: Build a personal portfolio website.
     - Objective: Showcase my web development skills and projects to potential employers.
     - SMART Goal: Launch a fully functional portfolio website with 5 projects and a contact form within 4 weeks.

2. **Target Audience:**
   - Who are you building this website for?
   - Understanding your audience helps shape design and content decisions.
   - **Example:**
     - Target Audience: Potential employers, recruiters, and fellow developers.

3. **Content Inventory:**
   - List all the content you need for the website.
   - This includes text, images, videos, and other media.

- ○ **Example:**
  - ■ Home page: Introduction, skills summary, featured projects.
  - ■ About page: Personal bio, skills list, resume download.
  - ■ Projects page: Project descriptions, screenshots, links to live demos.
  - ■ Contact page: Contact form, email address, social media links.

Structuring the Project

1. **Sitemap:**
   - ○ Create a visual representation of the website's structure.
   - ○ It helps you understand the hierarchy and navigation flow.
   - ○ **Example:**
   - ○ - Home
   - ○ - About
   - ○ - Projects
   - ○   - Project 1
   - ○   - Project 2
   - ○   - Project 3
   - ○ - Contact

Personal Insight: I always start with a sitemap. It helps me visualize the entire website and ensures a logical flow of information.

2. **Wireframes (Low-Fidelity):**
    - Create basic sketches of each page's layout.
    - Focus on content placement and functionality, not visual design.
    - **Example:**
        - Home page: Header with logo and navigation, hero section with introduction, featured projects section, footer.

3. **Design Mockups (High-Fidelity):**
    - Create detailed visual designs of each page using design tools like Figma or Adobe XD.
    - Include colors, typography, images, and other visual elements.
    - **Expert Commentary:** Design mockups bridge the gap between wireframes and the final product. They provide a clear visual representation of the website.

4. **Technology Stack:**
    - Choose the technologies you'll use for the project.
    - Consider factors like project requirements, performance, and development time.
    - **Example:**
        - HTML, CSS, JavaScript for front-end.
        - Node.js with Express.js for back-end (if needed).
        - Git for version control.
        - Hosting: Netlify or Vercel for static sites, Heroku or AWS for dynamic sites.

5. **Project Folder Structure:**
    - Organize your project files into a logical folder structure.
    - This makes it easier to manage and maintain the project.
    - **Example:**
    - my-portfolio/
    - ├── index.html
    - ├── about.html
    - ├── projects.html
    - ├── contact.html
    - ├── css/

- o | └── styles.css
- o ├── js/
- o | └── script.js
- o ├── images/
- o | └── project-1.jpg
- o └── README.md

Personal Insight: A well-organized folder structure is crucial, especially for larger projects. It saves time and prevents confusion.

6. **Timeline and Milestones:**
   - o Create a timeline with specific milestones.
   - o This helps you stay on track and manage your time effectively.
   - o **Example:**
     - Week 1: Project planning, wireframing, HTML structure.
     - Week 2: CSS styling, responsive design.
     - Week 3: JavaScript functionality, interactive elements.
     - Week 4: Testing, deployment, final adjustments.

Practical Implementation: Step-by-Step

1. **Define Project Goals and Audience:** Clearly outline what you want to achieve and who you're building for.
2. **Create a Content Inventory:** List all the content you need for the website.
3. **Develop a Sitemap:** Map out the website's structure and navigation.
4. **Create Wireframes and Mockups:** Design the layout and visual appearance of each page.

5. **Choose Your Technology Stack:** Select the technologies you'll use for the project.
6. **Set Up a Project Folder:** Create a logical folder structure for your files.
7. **Create a Timeline:** Set deadlines and milestones for your project.

8.2: Implementing Design and Functionality

This is where the magic happens! We'll translate our designs and plans into functional code.

Setting Up the Project Environment

1. **Create Project Files:**
   - Create HTML, CSS, and JavaScript files based on your project structure.
   - **Example:**
     - index.html, about.html, projects.html, contact.html
     - css/styles.css
     - js/script.js
2. **Link Files:**
   - Link your CSS and JavaScript files to your HTML files.
   - **Example (in <head> of HTML):**

HTML

```
<link rel="stylesheet" href="css/styles.css">
```

```
<script src="js/script.js" defer></script>
```

Personal Insight: Don't forget the defer attribute on your script tag. It ensures the script runs after the HTML is parsed, preventing potential errors.

Implementing the HTML Structure

1. **Semantic HTML:**
   - Use semantic HTML elements to structure your content.
   - **Example:**

HTML

```
<header>

    <nav>

        <ul>

            <li><a href="index.html">Home</a></li>

            <li><a href="about.html">About</a></li>
```

```html
          <li><a href="projects.html">Projects</a></li>

          <li><a href="contact.html">Contact</a></li>

        </ul>

      </nav>

  </header>

  <main>

    <section class="hero">

        <h1>Welcome to My Portfolio</h1>

        <p>Showcasing my web development skills and projects.</p>

    </section>
```

```
<section class="projects">


    <h2>Featured Projects</h2>


    </section>


</main>


<footer>


    <p>&copy; 2024 My Portfolio</p>


</footer>
```

2. **Content Placement:**
   - Place your content based on your wireframes and design mockups.
   - Use appropriate HTML elements for different types of content (headings, paragraphs, lists, images, etc.).

Styling with CSS

1. **CSS Reset/Normalize:**
   - ○ Use a CSS reset or normalize stylesheet to ensure consistent styling across browsers.
   - ○ **Example:**
     - ■ Include a reset or normalize stylesheet at the beginning of your styles.css file.
2. **Layout Styling:**
   - ○ Use CSS layout techniques (Flexbox, Grid) to create the desired layout.
   - ○ **Example (Flexbox):**

CSS

```css
header nav ul {



    display: flex;



  justify-content: center;}



header nav ul li {margin: 0 15px;}
```

Flexbox and Grid are powerful layout tools. Use them to create flexible and responsive designs.

3. **Visual Design:**
   - Apply colors, typography, and other visual styles based on your design mockups.
   - **Example:**

CSS

```
body {font-family: Arial, sans-serif;

   background-color: #f4f4f4}

h1 {   color: #333;   text-align: center;}

.hero {   background-color: #e0e0e0;

   padding: 50px;   text-align: center;}
```

4. **Responsive Design:**
   - Use media queries to create responsive designs that adapt to different screen sizes.
   - **Example:**

CSS

```
@media (max-width: 768px) { header nav ul {  flex-direction: column;
```

```
align-items: center; }header nav ul li {  margin: 10px 0;   }}
```

Adding JavaScript Functionality

1. **DOM Manipulation:**
   - Use JavaScript to manipulate the DOM and add interactivity.
   - **Example:**

JavaScript

```javascript
const hero = document.querySelector(".hero");
```

```javascript
hero.addEventListener("click", function() {  alert("Hero section clicked!");});
```

2. **Event Handling:**
   - Add event listeners to elements to respond to user interactions.
   - **Example:**

JavaScript

```javascript
const contactForm = document.getElementById("contact-form");

if (contactForm) {   contactForm.addEventListener("submit", function(event) {
event.preventDefault(); // Prevent form submission

    alert("Form submitted!");  });
```

3. **Interactive Elements:**
   - Implement interactive elements like modals, sliders, and form validation.
   - **Personal Insight:** Start with small, manageable JavaScript features. Gradually add more complex functionality as you progress.

Practical Implementation: Step-by-Step

1. **Set Up Project Files:** Create HTML, CSS, and JavaScript files.
2. **Link Files:** Link your CSS and JavaScript files to your HTML.
3. **Implement HTML Structure:** Use semantic HTML to structure your content.
4. **Style with CSS:** Apply visual styles and create responsive layouts.
5. **Add JavaScript Functionality:** Implement interactive elements and event handling.
6. **Test Thoroughly:** Test your website on different devices and browsers.

8.3: Testing, Deployment, and Maintenance

Launching a website is just the beginning. To ensure a successful and long-lasting online presence, you need to test thoroughly, deploy effectively, and maintain consistently.

Testing: Ensuring Quality and Functionality

1. **Cross-Browser Testing:**
   - Test your website on different browsers (Chrome, Firefox, Safari, Edge) to ensure consistent rendering and functionality.
   - **Tools:** BrowserStack, LambdaTest, or even just manually checking on different browsers.
   - **Personal Insight:** You'd be surprised how differently websites can look on different browsers. Cross-browser testing is a must.

2. **Responsive Testing:**
   - Test your website on various devices (desktops, tablets, smartphones) to ensure it adapts correctly to different screen sizes.
   - **Tools:** Browser developer tools, real devices, or online emulators.

3. **Usability Testing:**
   - Observe users as they interact with your website to identify usability issues.
   - **Methods:** User testing sessions, feedback forms, analytics.
   - **Expert Commentary:** Usability testing is invaluable for identifying blind spots. You'll see how real users interact, and often find things you never considered.

4. **Functionality Testing:**
   - Test all interactive elements (forms, buttons, links, etc.) to ensure they function as expected.
   - **Example:**
     - Test form submissions, navigation links, and JavaScript functionality.

5. **Performance Testing:**
   - Test your website's performance (loading speed, responsiveness) to identify and fix bottlenecks.
   - **Tools:** Google PageSpeed Insights, Lighthouse, WebPageTest.
   - **Personal Insight:** Performance is crucial. Even a few seconds of delay can drive users away.

6. **Accessibility Testing:**
   - Test your website's accessibility to ensure it's usable by people with disabilities.

- ○ **Tools:** WAVE, Axe, screen readers.
- ○ **Example:**
  - ■ Check for sufficient color contrast, keyboard navigation, and alternative text for images.

Deployment: Making Your Website Live

1. **Choose a Hosting Provider:**
   - ○ Select a hosting provider based on your project's requirements and budget.
   - ○ **Options:**
     - ■ **Static Sites:** Netlify, Vercel, GitHub Pages.
     - ■ **Dynamic Sites:** Heroku, AWS, Google Cloud, DigitalOcean.
2. **Set Up a Domain Name:**
   - ○ Register a domain name that reflects your brand or project.
   - ○ **Providers:** GoDaddy, Namecheap, Google Domains.
3. **Deploy Your Website:**
   - ○ Follow the hosting provider's instructions to deploy your website.
   - ○ **Example:**
     - ■ For Netlify, you can drag and drop your project folder or connect to a Git repository.[6]
     - ■ For Heroku, you can use the Heroku CLI to deploy your application.[7]
4. **Configure DNS Settings:**
   - ○ Point your domain name to your hosting provider's servers.
   - ○ This involves updating your DNS settings with your domain registrar.
5. **Set Up HTTPS:**
   - ○ Secure your website with an SSL certificate to enable HTTPS.
   - ○ Most hosting providers offer free SSL certificates.

Maintenance: Keeping Your Website Up-to-Date

1. **Regular Backups:**
   - Back up your website files and database regularly to prevent data loss.
   - **Methods:** Automatic backups through your hosting provider, manual backups.

2. **Software Updates:**
   - Keep your website's software and plugins up-to-date to ensure security and compatibility.
   - **Example:**
     - If you're using a CMS like WordPress, update the core software, themes, and plugins.

3. **Content Updates:**
   - Keep your website's content fresh and relevant.
   - **Example:**
     - Add new blog posts, update product information, and refresh images.

4. **Performance Monitoring:**
   - Monitor your website's performance and address any issues promptly.
   - **Tools:** Google Analytics, performance monitoring tools.

5. **Security Monitoring:**
   - Monitor your website for security vulnerabilities and take appropriate measures.
   - **Example:**
     - Use security plugins, update passwords, and monitor access logs.

6. **User Feedback:**
   - Collect and analyze user feedback to identify areas for improvement.
   - **Methods:** Feedback forms, surveys, analytics.

7. **SEO Maintenance:**
   - Continue to optimize your website for search engines.
   - **Example:**
     - Update meta tags, optimize content, and build backlinks.

Practical Implementation: Step-by-Step

1. **Test Thoroughly:** Conduct cross-browser, responsive, usability, functionality, performance, and accessibility testing.
2. **Choose a Hosting Provider:** Select a hosting provider that meets your needs.
3. **Set Up a Domain Name:** Register a domain name and configure DNS settings.
4. **Deploy Your Website:** Deploy your website to your hosting provider.
5. **Set Up HTTPS:** Secure your website with an SSL certificate.
6. **Create a Maintenance Plan:** Schedule regular backups, software updates, and content updates.
7. **Monitor Performance and Security:** Use tools to monitor your website's performance and security.
8. **Collect User Feedback:** Gather and analyze user feedback to improve your website.
9. **Maintain SEO:** Continue to optimize your website for search engines.

Chapter 9: Emerging Trends and Best Practices

The world of web design is constantly evolving. Staying up-to-date with the latest trends and best practices is essential for creating modern and effective websites.

9.1: Design Systems and Component Libraries

Design systems and component libraries are essential for building consistent and scalable user interfaces.They provide a standardized approach to design and development, promoting efficiency and collaboration.

Design Systems: The Blueprint for Consistency

A design system is a comprehensive guide for how a company or product should look and feel.It includes guidelines for visual design, interaction design, and content.

1. **Purpose:**
   - To ensure consistency across all products and platforms.
   - To improve collaboration between designers and developers.
   - To accelerate the design and development process.
2. **Key Elements:**
   - **Visual Style Guide:** Defines colors, typography, spacing, and iconography.
   - **Component Library:** A collection of reusable UI components.
   - **Interaction Guidelines:** Defines how users interact with the UI.
   - **Content Guidelines:** Defines voice, tone, and writing style.
   - **Design Principles:** Defines the core values and goals of the design.
   - **Documentation:** Provides clear and concise documentation for all aspects of the design system.
   - **Personal Insight:** A design system is like a style guide on steroids. It's not just about visuals; it's about creating a cohesive user experience.
3. **Example (Visual Style Guide):**

- Colors:
  - Primary: #007bff
  - Secondary: #6c757d
  - Success: #28a745
  - Error: #dc3545
- Typography:
  - Font Family: Arial, sans-serif
  - Headings: font-weight: bold; font-size: 2rem;
  - Body Text: font-size: 1rem; line-height: 1.5;
- Spacing:
  - Padding: 8px, 16px, 24px
  - Margin: 8px, 16px, 24px

Component Libraries: Reusable UI Elements

A component library is a collection of reusable UI components that can be used across different projects.It promotes code reusability and consistency.

1. **Purpose:**
   - To create a library of reusable UI components.
   - To improve development efficiency.
   - To ensure consistency across different projects.
2. **Key Elements:**
   - **Buttons:** Primary, secondary, outline.
   - **Forms:** Input fields, checkboxes, radio buttons.
   - **Navigation:** Menus, tabs, breadcrumbs.
   - **Cards:** Containers for content.
   - **Modals:** Pop-up windows.
   - **Alerts:** Notifications.

- Documentation: Provides clear and concise documentation for each component.[12]
- Expert Commentary: Component libraries are a developer's best friend. They save time and ensure consistency.

3. **Example (Button Component):**
   - **HTML:**

```
<button class="button button-primary">Primary Button</button>

<button class="button button-secondary">Secondary Button</button>13

```
```

- CSS:```css.button {padding: 10px 20px; border: none;border-radius: 5px; cursor: pointer; font-size: 1rem;}.button-primary { background-color: #007bff; color: white;}.button-secondary {background-color: #6c757d;   color: white;}```

4. **Framework Integration:**
   - Component libraries are often built using JavaScript frameworks like React, Vue.js, or Angular.
   - **Example (React):**

JavaScript

```
// Button.jsxfunction Button({ children, className, ...props }) {return ( <button className={`button ${className}`} {...props}> {children} </button> );}export default Button;// Usage:<Button className="button-primary">Click Me</Button>
```

116
```

Practical Implementation: Step-by-Step

1. **Define Design Principles:** Establish the core values and goals of your design.
2. **Create a Visual Style Guide:** Define colors, typography, spacing, and iconography.
3. **Build a Component Library:** Create reusable UI components using HTML, CSS, and JavaScript.
4. **Document Your Design System:** Provide clear and concise documentation for all aspects of the design system.
5. **Implement the Design System:** Apply the design system to your projects.
6. **Maintain and Update:** Regularly review and update the design system to ensure it remains relevant.

Key Considerations:

- **Collaboration:** Involve designers and developers in the creation and maintenance of the design system.
- **Accessibility:** Ensure all components are accessible to users with disabilities.
- **Scalability:** Design the system to be scalable and adaptable to future needs.
- **Version Control:** Use version control to track changes to the design system.

9.2: Performance Optimization and Security

Performance and security are critical aspects of modern web development. A fast and secure website not only enhances user experience but also builds trust and credibility.

Performance Optimization: Speeding Up Your Website

1. **Code Optimization:**
   - **Minification:** Remove unnecessary characters (spaces, line breaks) from your CSS and JavaScript files.

- **Compression:** Compress files using Gzip or Brotli to reduce their size.
- **Code Splitting:** Break down your JavaScript code into smaller chunks that are loaded on demand.
- **Example:**
  - Use tools like UglifyJS for JavaScript minification and CSSNano for CSS minification.
  - Configure your server to enable Gzip or Brotli compression.
  - **Personal Insight:** Code splitting can significantly improve initial load times, especially for large applications.

2. **Image Optimization:**
   - **Compression:** Compress images without sacrificing too much quality.
   - **Responsive Images:** Use the \<picture\> element or srcset attribute to serve different image sizes based on screen size.
   - **Lazy Loading:** Load images only when they are visible in the viewport.
   - **Modern Formats:** Use WebP or AVIF formats for better compression.
   - **Example:**
     - Use tools like TinyPNG or ImageOptim for image compression.
     - Use the loading="lazy" attribute on \<img\> elements.
     - **Expert Commentary:** Image optimization is often overlooked, but it can have a huge impact on performance.

3. **Caching:**
   - **Browser Caching:** Leverage browser caching to store static assets (images, CSS, JavaScript) in the user's browser.
   - **CDN (Content Delivery Network):** Use a CDN to distribute your website's assets across multiple servers.
   - **Server-Side Caching:** Implement caching on your server to store frequently accessed data.
   - **Example:**
     - Configure your server to set appropriate cache headers.
     - Use a CDN like Cloudflare or Amazon CloudFront.

4. **Minimize HTTP Requests:**
   - ○ Reduce the number of HTTP requests by combining files and using CSS sprites.
   - ○ **Example:**
     - ■ Combine multiple CSS or JavaScript files into a single file.
     - ■ Use CSS sprites to combine multiple images into a single image.

5. **Performance Auditing:**
   - ○ Use tools like Google PageSpeed Insights, Lighthouse, or WebPageTest to analyze website performance.
   - ○ Identify and fix performance bottlenecks.
   - ○ **Personal Insight:** Regularly auditing your website's performance is crucial.It helps you identify and address issues before they impact users.

Security: Protecting Your Website and Users

1. **HTTPS:**
   - ○ Use HTTPS to encrypt communication between the browser and the server.
   - ○ **Example:**
     - ■ Obtain an SSL certificate from a trusted provider.
     - ■ Configure your server to use HTTPS.

2. **Input Validation:**
   - ○ Validate user input to prevent malicious code injection.
   - ○ **Example:**
     - ■ Sanitize user input before storing it in the database.
     - ■ Use server-side validation to prevent client-side bypasses.

3. **Cross-Site Scripting (XSS) Protection:**
   - ○ Sanitize user-generated content to prevent XSS attacks.
   - ○ **Example:**

- Use appropriate encoding and escaping techniques.
- Set the Content-Security-Policy header.

4. **Cross-Site Request Forgery (CSRF) Protection:**
   - Use CSRF tokens to prevent unauthorized requests.
   - **Example:**
     - Generate and validate CSRF tokens on the server.

5. **Secure Authentication and Authorization:**
   - Use strong passwords and multi-factor authentication.
   - Implement proper authorization mechanisms to control access to resources.
   - **Example:**
     - Use bcrypt or Argon2 for password hashing.
     - Implement role-based access control (RBAC).

6. **Regular Security Updates:**
   - Keep your software and plugins up-to-date to patch security vulnerabilities.
   - **Example:**
     - Regularly update your operating system, web server, and application frameworks.

7. **Security Audits and Penetration Testing:**
   - Conduct regular security audits and penetration testing to identify and fix security vulnerabilities.
   - **Personal Insight:** Security is an ongoing process. Stay informed about the latest security threats and best practices.

Practical Implementation: Step-by-Step

1. **Optimize Code:** Minify, compress, and split your code.
2. **Optimize Images:** Compress, resize, and use modern image formats.
3. **Implement Caching:** Leverage browser caching, CDNs, and server-side caching.
4. **Minimize HTTP Requests:** Combine files and use CSS sprites.

5. **Perform Performance Audits:** Use tools to analyze and optimize your website's performance.
6. **Implement HTTPS:** Secure your website with an SSL certificate.
7. **Validate User Input:** Sanitize and validate user input.
8. **Protect Against XSS and CSRF:** Use appropriate encoding and tokens.
9. **Implement Secure Authentication and Authorization:** Use strong passwords and proper access control.
10. **Regular Security Updates:** Keep your software and plugins up-to-date.
11. **Conduct Security Audits:** Regularly audit and test your website's security.

9.3: The Future of Web Design: Innovations

The web is ever-evolving, and staying ahead of the curve is crucial.Let's look at some key innovations shaping the future of web design.

1. AI and Machine Learning in Web Design

1. **Personalized Experiences:**
    - AI can analyze user behavior and preferences to deliver personalized content and recommendations.
    - **Example:**
        - E-commerce sites using AI to suggest products based on browsing history.
        - News websites tailoring content based on user interests.
2. **Automated Design Tools:**
    - AI-powered tools can generate design layouts, color palettes, and typography based on user input.
    - **Example:**
        - AI-driven website builders that create responsive designs automatically.
        - Tools that generate UI components based on design specifications.
3. **Chatbots and Virtual Assistants:**

- ○ AI-powered chatbots can provide instant customer support and answer user queries.
- ○ **Example:**
  - ■ Websites using chatbots to handle common customer service requests.
  - ■ Virtual assistants that guide users through website navigation.
- ○ **Personal Insight:** AI is poised to revolutionize user interaction.It's about making the web more intuitive and responsive.

2. Progressive Web Apps (PWAs)

1. **App-Like Experiences:**
   - ○ PWAs provide app-like experiences within the browser, offering features like offline access, push notifications, and home screen installation.
   - ○ **Example:**
     - ■ Twitter Lite, Pinterest, and Starbucks PWAs.
2. **Improved Performance:**
   - ○ PWAs are designed to be fast and responsive, providing a seamless user experience.
   - ○ **Expert Commentary:** PWAs bridge the gap between websites and native apps.They're perfect for mobile-first experiences.

3. WebAssembly (Wasm)

1. **Near-Native Performance:**
   - ○ Wasm allows developers to run code written in languages like C++, Rust, and Go in the browser at near-native speed.
   - ○ **Example:**
     - ■ Running complex games and applications in the browser.

- Using Wasm to improve the performance of computationally intensive tasks.

2. **Expanded Possibilities:**
   - Wasm opens up new possibilities for web development, allowing developers to bring desktop-level performance to the web.
   - **Personal Insight:** Wasm is a game-changer for web performance. It's about unlocking the full potential of the browser.

4. 3D and Immersive Experiences

1. **WebXR:**
   - WebXR allows developers to create immersive virtual reality (VR) and augmented reality (AR) experiences in the browser.
   - **Example:**
     - Virtual product try-ons, interactive 3D models, and immersive training simulations.

2. **3D Graphics:**
   - 3D graphics are becoming more common on the web, enhancing user engagement and interactivity.
   - **Example:**
     - Interactive 3D product visualizations, virtual tours, and 3D animations

5. Voice User Interfaces (VUIs)

1. **Voice Interaction:**
   - VUIs allow users to interact with websites and applications using voice commands.

- Example:
    - Voice-activated search, voice navigation, and voice-controlled forms.
2. **Accessibility:**
    - VUIs can improve accessibility for users with disabilities.

6. Serverless Architecture

1. **Scalability and Efficiency:**
    - Serverless architecture allows developers to build and deploy applications without managing servers.
    - **Example:**
        - Using serverless functions to handle API requests and background tasks.
2. **Cost-Effectiveness:**
    - Serverless architecture can reduce infrastructure costs and improve scalability.

7. Design Systems and Design Tokens

1. **Scalability and Consistency:**
    - Design systems and design tokens are becoming more sophisticated, allowing for greater scalability and consistency across large projects.
    - **Example:**
        - Using design tokens to manage colors, typography, and spacing across different platforms.
2. **Improved Collaboration:**
    - Design systems and design tokens improve collaboration between designers and developers.

Practical Considerations:

- **Continuous Learning:** Stay up-to-date with the latest web technologies and trends.
- **Experimentation:** Don't be afraid to experiment with new technologies and techniques.
- **User-Centered Approach:** Always keep the user's needs and goals in mind.
- **Accessibility:** Ensure new technologies are accessible to everyone.
- **Performance:** Prioritize performance in all aspects of web development.

Conclusion: Your Web Design Journey Continues

We've reached the end of our journey through the world of web design, and I hope you're feeling empowered and inspired to create amazing websites. We've covered a lot of ground, from the fundamental building blocks of HTML, CSS, and JavaScript to advanced techniques like responsive design, interactivity, and modern workflows.

Reflecting on Our Journey

Remember when we first started? We explored the core principles of web design, understanding the importance of user experience (UX) and user interface (UI). We learned how to structure content with HTML, style it with CSS, and add interactivity with JavaScript. We delved into responsive design, ensuring our websites look great on any device. We even explored advanced topics like CSS preprocessors, asynchronous JavaScript, and the exciting possibilities of design systems and emerging technologies.

The Power of Practice

Throughout this book, I've emphasized the importance of practice. Web design is a skill that improves with experience. Don't be afraid to experiment, make mistakes, and learn from them. Every website you build will teach you something new.

My Personal Takeaway

Writing this book has been a fantastic experience for me. It's allowed me to reflect on my own journey as a web developer and share the lessons I've learned along the way. I've realized that web design is not just about writing code; it's about solving problems, creating experiences, and communicating ideas.

The Web is Your Canvas

The web is a vast and ever-evolving canvas. There's always something new to learn and explore. Whether you're building a personal portfolio, a blog, an e-commerce store, or a complex web application, the possibilities are endless.

Key Reminders:

- **User-Centered Approach:** Always keep the user in mind. Design for their needs and goals.
- **Continuous Learning:** The web is constantly changing. Stay curious and keep learning.
- **Practice, Practice, Practice:** The more you build, the better you'll become.
- **Embrace Community:** Connect with other web developers, share your knowledge, and learn from each other.
- **Accessibility Matters:** Build websites that are accessible to everyone.
- **Performance is Key:** Optimize your websites for speed and efficiency.

Your Next Steps

Now that you've completed this book, here are some suggestions for your next steps:

- **Build Your Portfolio:** Create a portfolio website to showcase your skills and projects.
- **Contribute to Open Source:** Contribute to open-source projects to gain experience and collaborate with other developers.
- **Explore Frameworks:** Dive deeper into frameworks like React, Vue.js, or Angular.
- **Stay Updated:** Follow blogs, podcasts, and social media accounts to stay up-to-date with the latest trends.
- **Never Stop Learning:** The journey of a web developer is a lifelong learning experience.

Thank You!

Thank you for joining me on this adventure! I hope this book has provided you with the knowledge and inspiration you need to pursue your web design goals. Remember, the web is your canvas, and you have the power to create amazing things.